Tra...

Light-Hearted and Enlightening World Travel

Volume 2: Rambles in Europe

By

Gary Zacny

Copyright 2019 by Gary Zacny

ISBN: 9781082724176

Foreword

My first volume of travelogues offered the casual reader a few pleasant, I hope, journeys of the imagination. Also, it had a few points to make, or at least it had a question to answer. It was my attempt to puzzle out, via anecdotes, chance encounters and a kaleidoscope of travel experiences, the ways and means in which various ancient cultures wrought what we call "civilization". What produced the dominion of Egypt, the grandeur of Greece, the glory of Rome?

This volume has no such theme. It's just for fun. Travel ought to be more than moving our protoplasm from place to place, and armchair travel ought to be more than leafing through travel brochures. It should be educational, amusing and inspiring enough to make us come back for more.

During my rambles about Europe, my habit has been to turn people-watching, place-gazing, and history-browsing into a running commentary on the look and feel and character of Europe as presents itself today, with a few reflections on how it got to be that way. Travel gives us a chance to marvel at the endless beauties of the natural world and the endless diversity of human society. Seeing the sights, walking the walks, just being there – travel illuminates both the traveler and his or her place in the larger world.

I hope you find it fun. The book has done some good if it makes you want to get up and go see for yourself.

--Gary

Travel Light, Volume 2: Rambles in Europe

Table of Contents

Foreword 3

Northern Italy 6

    Venice 8
    Florence.. 20
    Tuscany 26
    Pisa.. 30
    Portofino 33
    Italian Lake Region 36
    Italian Renaissance.................................. 40

France 43

    Normandy... 43
    Giverny 44
    Bayeaux.. 46
    Normandy Beachhead............................... 48
    Bayeaux Tapestry..................................... 51
    Barfleur 53
    Mont St. Michel 59
    St. Malo 64
    Brittany.. 67
    Loire River Valley 71
    Chartres... 84
    Paris 86
    Basel.. 92
    Dublin and Surroundings......................... 101
    James Joyce Tower.................................. 104
    Book of Kells 107

England 111

    London 111
    Smith's Meat Market 115
    Bloomsbury 122
    British Museum 126
    Piccadilly Circus....................................... 129
    Drive on the Left You Fool 130
    Winchester 134

Oxford.. 140
Warwick.. 145
Stonehenge... 150
Bath 154
Portsmouth.. 158

The View from Across the Pond 162

Northern Italy

For God and for profit.
  -- motto of the Medici bank

In my youth Italy arrived as an undigested and indigestible garbage pizza of images and ideas: Columbus sailed the ocean blue, Perry Como crooning on late night television, the movies <u>Sahara</u> and <u>Spartacus</u>, spaghetti and spumoni, and the humble immigrant in <u>It's A Wonderful Life</u> who opens a restaurant in pursuit of the American Dream. None of it made much sense, and somehow it never made a deep impression later in my studies, pushed aside by the Russians and sputnik and, of course, girls.

I felt a gap in my education bigger than a missing tooth. I felt a need to understand whatever became of the good old Roman Empire. I felt a hunger to experience Italy because it was the re-birthplace of the Renaissance, a recurring theme of my travels, a place where some lucky combination of bountiful land and national character made for another spectacular flowering of human intellect. It seemed like a good idea to go there and to sample the culture that spawned Leonardo, Michelangelo, and the rest. Not to mention the pizza.

My wife Ellen was agreeable, although her interest in Italy was based more on opera, cathedrals and a luridly romantic film called <u>Under the Tuscan Sun</u>. Accordingly we studied a few guidebooks to Italy and she bought a few maps and we laid plans to drive through northern Italy, mainly Venice and Florence with possible stops in Padua, Bologna, Siena, Genoa and Como. That was the plan, but, as a Scottish bard has said, "The best laid plans of mice and men gang aft aglay."

On the connecting flight from Chicago to Paris they showed a new movie called <u>The Devil Made me Wear Prada</u>, or something like that – a comedy about the intensely competitive world of high fashion, filled with images of rich clothes and dolled-up people. This was to become a leitmotiv of our Italian travels, since the streets of Milan and Venice and Florence overflowed with women in designer jeans and men in smart Armani jackets. We developed a Prada-scale to discuss the flow of chic people. A woman in black crepe mini-skirt and thigh-high leather boots was an 8.5 on the Prada-scale, and a man in crumpled corduroy trousers and spaghetti-flecked tie was a minus 2 on the Prada-scale. Most of the *haute couture* statements were lost on me, since I am a guy whose idea of fashion is light-shirt-with-dark-pants and dark-shirt-with-light-pants, and to me a skinny girl in polka dot jodhpurs looks simply outlandish. Repeatedly this parade of high fashion chockablock with Donatello and Michelangelo raised questions about the distinction between fashion and art which I could not answer. All I know is this: Michelangelo's David wears nothing at all and he looks just fine.

Venice

We landed in Milan but almost immediately jumped in a rental car and headed east for Venice. Rain fell in fits and mists as we drove through northeastern Italy, the region of Alps-fed lakes and hill country in the Venetian Arc. When we emerged from tunnels in the foothills, sunlight broke from gray clouds to reveal vineyards and olive groves and green fields. We got lost or distracted around Sirmione. (This was to become a continuing technique of our travels – to be caught up in conversation and so to miss or misunderstand road signage and to get slightly lost and happen upon out-of-the-way Italy). We stopped beside Lake

Garda where still gray waters stretched into faint gray mist. In the distance scattered waterfowl sailed on a silver mirror, and around us silence hung in the heavy air.

We found a local *trattoria* (smaller than a *ristorante* but with a larger menu than a café or *osteria*, and enlivened often with local cuisine). Ellen had wild boar and I had beef marinated in red wine. The meal highlight was the polenta, a sort of cornmeal mush, only this time baked as a loaf and served as slices under gravy. Our waitress, and probably also proprietor and cook, accepted compliments on the meal (*squisito* or exquisite), happy for company in the off-season, rainy day, odd hour, deserted little inn.

We arrived at the Adriatic coast with plenty of daylight left, according to plan. We parked in the remote lot, as recommended by Fodor's Italy, and lugged our luggage to the ferry dock. The last ferry for the day had just left. We got lost promptly and drove around the bus station lot three or four times and failed to find a parking lot near the train station and in frustration headed over the causeway to park (at 20 € per day) near the bus terminal. I asked a taxi driver in pidgin Italian if he could help us reach Venice. He sighed, shook his head sadly and replied, "Venice all water. Is no cars."

We trundled our preposterously large suitcases to the dock, caught a water taxi to the Castello region of the city, and walked up and down bridges, through innumerable winding passageways, asking directions of kind strangers all the way until we reached our obscure little hotel. Before the trip started I had booked tickets to a concert that evening of "The Four Seasons" by Vivaldi, performed by a Venetian chamber orchestra. When we flopped on the hotel room bed, sweaty, bone weary, and sleep deprived, we had less than an hour to navigate the labyrinthine city to a quaint, obscure theatre.

We surrendered to Venice instead and unpacked, showered, changed and followed the concierge's directions to a local *ristorante* to enjoy pasta – in this instance spaghetti with asparagus and prawns – followed by sea bass and a smooth local Verona Soave Superiore. In my heart I said "To Hell with Vivaldi."

Morning sunlight streamed into the room at the elegant seven-room hotel called Ca'Bauta (House of The Mask). Exposed wooden beams ran across high recessed ceilings. Silk curtains fell gracefully from 20-foot high windows. Period furniture upholstered in striped silk and ornate carved wooden tables adorned the spacious room. Marco Polo would have felt at home. Church bells rang from the nearby Dominican church known as Santa Giovanni e Paolo. The air was fresh and faintly salt-laced, the sky a piercing blue, the hibiscus vivid red, and the tile rooftops below the window gleaming terra-cotta. Ah, Venice and *la dolce vita!*

The courtyard of Ca'Bauta had a palm tree. Just outside the gate I snapped pictures of a mustard-colored stucco building with fresh laundry hanging on a line between buildings.

A few steps down the narrow, cobbled passageway and a turn onto a larger pedestrian passage stood a produce stand with lush green beans, a vegetable shaped like a squid, fresh artichokes, perfect strawberries and plums and tomatoes.

I had heard that the light in Venice is special, an observation I dismissed as romantic fancy, but this first morning I discovered it was true. Something about the way sunlight reflects from the surrounding glittering sea, and the morning and evening mists, and the dappled light bouncing off the canals creates a strange effect of light simultaneously muted and brilliant.

We made our way west toward the famous Piazza San Marco, passing countless shops with Versace and Gucci accessories, taverns decked in wine bottles, gelato stands and the usual pharmacies and cell phone stores. One shop had a window display of bright fanciful masks, some shaped like

Pinocchio and some like beasts, some feathered and some sequined, all dedicated to Carnival and the elaborate, elegant frivolity for which Venice is famed. Many shops featured colorful glass objects from craft shops on the nearby island of Murano. The glass wine stoppers and beads and paperweights sparkled in the morning sunlight. I liked especially a glass ball shaped like a fishbowl with blue shading at the bottom and at the center a tiny glass goldfish.

We took the *vaporetto* (water bus) Number 1 along the Grand Canal. Quaint stucco buildings flowed past in a tan and pink procession. The ground floor at water level on many buildings is stained, apparently from occasional flooding, and in places the stucco has washed away to reveal the brickwork underneath. Ornamentation on the bottom floor is scant compared to the plaster curlicues and Romanesque windows of the upper floors. People thronged the piazzas and the canal-side cafes. Lively traffic plied the frosted gray waters of the Grand Canal. The watercraft included lots of tourist gondolas, yes, but also sturdy yellow water taxis (*traghetto*) and water ambulances and water bread trucks.

The American humorist Fred Allen once landed a job for the *New York Times* as a foreign correspondent stationed in Venice. When he arrived at his new assignment he wired his boss: ARRIVED VENICE THIS A.M. STOP STREETS FILLED WITH WATER STOP PLEASE ADVISE

Emerging from the dark labyrinthine streets into Piazza San Marco (St. Mark's Square), we beheld the huge Byzantine cathedral (Basilica di San Marco) and the city hall tower topped with a winged lion, and, to our delight, a flood. The expansive square was covered with two or three inches of sea water. A long line of tourists stood on portable raised walkways about a foot above the flood. We thought that a flood at the basilica was a jolly and amusing spectacle, something to write home about, and I snapped pictures of people wading the shallows and jostling on the raised walkways. Later in the trip we learned that this was a routine event. All the sidewalk cafes had procedures to pull their tiny tables and chairs up from the surge, and the raised walkways were commonly stored in alleys, and people nonchalantly waded across the wet brick square.

The second day in Venice, a Sunday, I had also pre-arranged tickets to a musical event, a genuine Italian opera to be performed at the opera house known as Teatro de Fenice. We left a little early but, per our traveling technique, got lost and arrived a little late so that we had to take our seats in the dark. Only after settling into our second-row box seats did I discover that I could not see the stage. I was flummoxed. Box seats, the best available on the web site and more than a hundred Euros per butt, and not even a view of the stage! Apparently in the antique theatres of Venice, unlike the Lyric Opera House in Chicago, a box seat is a place not to see but to be seen. By scrunching forward and craning, Ellen was able to see the performance, an authentic period piece with singers in silk-flounced dresses and periwigs. I could make out period instruments in the orchestra pit: 11 violins, 3 cellos, two French horns without valves, two long-necked mandolins, a bass and a double spinet used for percussion. The opera was *L'Olimpiade* by Baldassare Galuppi, a sprightly comedy about star-crossed lovers in the time of the ancient Olympics, but of course, the plot makes no sense in opera anyway. Ellen tells me it was delightful, and the voices very fine, but I leaned back in my chair, closed my eyes and dozed. The bloomin' thing lasted four hours and sixteen minutes. In my fashion I enjoyed the opera very much. I would recommend a CD of that opera to the medical community, to be prescribed for patients who are having trouble falling asleep. Call it a "soperaific."

We got lost (naturally) meandering back to the hotel. But the streets were safe, patrolled by men in natty gray uniforms, and the welcome lights of little *trattoria* glowed in pleasant mild air. Dinner was *gnocchi* (potato dumplings) in meat sauce, grilled vegetables and a solid Tokai wine.

The next day brought a walking tour of Venice. Crossing the Grand Canal on the Rialto Bridge and ducking through sprawling cafes, past countless boutiques and shoe stores, we emerged on the now familiar Piazza San Marco. The five plump domes of the basilica, like upside-down garlic bulbs, have a vaguely Turkish look, befitting a city that, since the time of Marco Polo, served as the crossroads of Europe and the Orient. Years ago, I read the journals of Marco Polo, a fascinating account of opening the Silk Road that brought spices, silk, pasta, chess and a hundred wonders of China to the benighted folks of Europe.   The thing that most impressed Marco Polo was the communication system of the Chinese Emperor. The emperor set up hundreds of relay stations with fast horses and skilled riders at each post, so that a message could be sent Pony Express-style across his vast empire in less than a day. The system astounded Marco Polo and served to underline for him the inferiority of medieval European governments.

Late on another golden afternoon we stopped in the bone dry Piazza San Marco. We were enjoying the *passeggiata*, a fine Italian term for a procession without a destination. Ellen bought a bag of popcorn kernels from a handy kiosk and was immediately surrounded by hundreds of the thousands of pigeons that swarm the piazza. They landed on her shoulders, her hair, and her outstretched arms. They pecked gently at the palms holding the corn. At first the sight of a bird perched on a head seemed comical, but later I decided that the feathered topper was charming and probably the inspiration for those 19th Century dove-like hats. The pigeons left on one's shoulders a fine white powder, a combination of sea salt, corn fluff and pulverized bird shit.

Tuesday brought a gloomy gray sky, and a good day to oversleep and luxuriate in the hotel dining salon. Everywhere in Italy they included breakfast with the hotel room, and the breakfast included thick espresso coffee with a little pitcher of warm milk. Very civilized. We lollygagged at breakfast, enjoying what the Italians call *il dolce far niente*, "the sweetness of doing nothing."

We were learning how to navigate the city. We zoomed straight north, caught a *vaporetto* and headed for the glass craft shops of Murano Island. But on the way to Murano we mistakenly (naturally) got off at an earlier stop and found ourselves at Cimitiere, the city cemetery. It was a happy accident because the cemetery of Venice, like the cemeteries of America's sub-sea-level city New Orleans, consists of innumerable above-ground vaults with elaborate memorials and mausoleums and statues. It was like a solemn art museum. One section of Cimitiere was devoted to the military, another to craft guilds and still others dedicated to old families of the maritime republic. A sign near the Slavic section pointed toward "Igor Strawinski" and I thought we had stumbled on the composer's grave. But later I earned that Stravinski was buriedInstead we encountered a small shrine dedicated to a Polish ballerina, engraved with sheet music and displaying dainty ballet slippers in marble.

Murano Island is now mostly residential, with just a small shopping area and museum near the dock. The Glass Museum told the story of glass making:

> 1) glass manufacture is an ancient and simple process -- just heat sand to 7000 degrees and catch the drippings
>
> 2) Venice became the European center for the industry due to a riverbed containing especially pure sand
>
> 3) the Venetians feared that glass-making furnaces would burn down their city and so they moved the whole kit and caboodle -- furnaces and warehouses and glassblowers -- to the nearby island of Murano

17

4) over centuries the craft progressed by trial and error, successively inventing techniques to color and cut and fuse and shape melted silica. The museum contained room after room of glass extravaganzas, swirled vases and sparkling crystal bowls and delicate glass chandeliers.

We stopped for lunch including a decent local wine, Bardolino, and then the glass shops proved irresistible. We came away with assorted doo-dads like beads and glass eggs and gold-frosted ruby Christmas ornaments. My prize was a flock of tiny glass penguins, each perfectly detailed and the size of a pencil eraser. They would look fine marching across the snowy landscape of a white linen tablecloth.

Hurriedly we jumped aboard the next *traghetto*, chugged across a slip of the Adriatic, dallied at a museum display of 18th Century costume, bustled through streets now dotted with familiar landmarks (left at the Church of St Giovanni-Paolo-Giorggio-Ringo, right at the winery with the dragon-shaped sign, another right at the Armani store with the austere manikin in metallic gold hot-pants, over the little bridge and past the gondola stand). We bought tickets from the concierge and zoomed to yet another neighborhood to discover a tiny concert hall, exactly the size of Pieta Hall where Vivaldi gave his premieres. Vivaldi is a home-town boy, and his music and image are splashed about Venice like cheap cologne. Earlier we had stumbled upon one store that offered nothing but Vivaldi – books and posters and racks of CDs featuring "The Four Seasons" by groups Venetian, Milanese, French, Dutch, German and American. Somewhere in that store I bet there is a recording of "The Four Seasons" played on tuba, tambourine and combs with tissue paper.

The concert was excellent. The intimate music hall was packed with about 100 people who listened as just five instruments, a soprano and a tenor performed arias by Vivaldi, Puccini, Donizetti, Bizet and Verdi. All in all, a gracious setting for gracious entertainment. In my heart I said "Bravo, Vivaldi". The music was so good that I hardly slept.

We headed back to Piazza San Marco and found three orchestras playing light classics and show tunes in the open air. At the piano bar they served a fine Bellini in a fluted glass, a fragrant froth of champagne and crushed peaches. When one orchestra struck up a Viennese waltz, the crowd would wander over there, and after a few tunes the next orchestra would break into a Sondheim tune, and the crowd would sidle toward them. We stayed at the back and danced a slow foxtrot on the brick pavement while moonlight and evening mist softened streetlights into a glowing dandelion haze.

Tuesday we slept late, had a muzzy breakfast, packed and began the dreaded trudge back to the mainland and the car. It turned out to be not all that bad, and we got to the boat dock without getting lost once. The captain of the little tugboat, however, told us not to board. Something about much water and no access and a shrug. A kind Venetian lady suggested that we take the next ferry in the opposite direction (#62), and so we headed counter-clockwise around nearly the whole island and discovered en route that high tide had arrived just as we started to depart. At restaurants the *al fresco* chairs sat in two or three feet of water. Saltwater lapped at ground floor windows and rolled into courtyards. Some of the women wore stylish calf-high rubber boots. About a 7.5 on the Prada-scale. Ellen remarked that Venice is the only city where you have to check the tide tables to know what to wear to work.

With a pang, as the skyline of Venice receded in the distance, I realized that I forgot to take a gondola ride. Ye gads, how can a person visit Venice and not ride a gondola? And then, just as suddenly, I didn't care. I had watched the tourists stepping into the peapod boats – a Japanese guy with dangling cameras that bumped the gunwales, a middle-aged couple, still bickering, plopping down on faux leopard skin cushions, a couple of women on a girls' vacation vaguely embarrassed to be handed into the boat by gondoliers, but determined to sample this staple of romance. And I decided that a gondola ride was simply hokey, strictly Disneyland, as phony as the loneliness of gondoliers in loud striped shirts trying to sing "O solo mio". For me the real romance of Venice will be music at midnight drifting over Piazza San Marco and bellinis and soft laughter in the thickening air while we danced in the moonlight.

Florence

The drive south toward Florence brought bright blue skies and green hills. At the ancient university town of Padua we lunched on the riverbank. The students of Padua ambled past us, dressed in shabby jeans, black t-shirts and gym shoes. My *panini* (grilled sandwich) contained the excellent *prosciutto* (air-cured ham) of the region. I liked the way the kids dressed, a style that deliberately scorns style, indistinguishable from the students back home, a trans-ethnic, quasi-universal, one-world style of ragged jeans and black tops and backpacks. We sat munching on the riverbank while the students streamed by above, in black, and the swans streamed by below, in white.

Further south we left Emilia-Romagna, the land of Parma and parmesan cheese and tangy balsamic vinegar. At the outskirts of Florence here at the end of October the mottled forested hills turned colors. The hills were dotted with foliage colored butter yellow, lemon, mustard, terra-cotta, coral and cranberry. A light rain began to fall and at the gas station I watched drifting rain clouds snag on hilltops and spill down like taffeta waterfalls. It reminded me of the way clouds just west of San Francisco spill over the mountains into the Bay.

I had a devil of a time finding the hotel in Florence, which was just around the corner from Ponte Vecchio, and so it should have been easy to locate. Around the sturdy little rental car motorcycles buzzed like angry bees. Narrow streets and swarming traffic and honking drivers made the search for a hotel a long, nerve-wracking struggle. After we got settled, a glass or two of wine helped soothe my nerves. Then we strolled to a sidewalk *osteria* and had a little more of the local wine, the ubiquitous Chianti. Ellen had a pork steak, called oddly a *bistecca*, and I had chicken *florentina*, a bird smothered in tomato sauce and black olives. Then another stroll north of the Arno River to watch an Arab band plunk out jazz tunes on bass, dulcimer, accordion and bongos. Then another local specialty, the bitter orange liqueur called Campari, served with soda and a lemon slice at a quiet bar.

Wednesday was for walking. We walked to the marble-clad San Giovanni Basillica and admired Ghiberti's bronze Doors of Paradise. We walked around the glorious cathedral of Florence, the Cattedrale di Santa Maria del Fiore (Our Lady of the Flower) with the graceful terra-cotta-tiled dome (Duomo). We walked up all 414 steps of the bell tower or Campanile. We walked across the Arno on the old bridge Ponte Vecchio and browsed the jewelry shops. We walked past the office buildings (Uffizi) erected by the Medici family and now used to house one of Europe's finest art collections. We admired the statue reproductions in the square, and we lingered a half hour hoping to scan-browse the giant museum, but the queue was too long, so we rode a one-horse carriage back uptown to the Gallerie d'ell Acadamie to see Michelangelo's statue of David.

I had seen the *David* and the Uffizi on a previous visit to Florence, and I remember feeling foolish to discover that the figure's odd posture, that powerful slouch, was explained by the fact that David had a sling slung over his shoulder. And I remember admiring the unfinished Michelangelo statues of the entryway and how the figures seemed intensely human in their struggle to emerge from the stone. This trip I really looked into David's eyes, and I came away haunted by the clarity of his gaze. This statue is often described as the quintessence of the Renaissance, the emblem of the emerging humanism that rocked Florence and subsequently the world. On this viewing I saw David's stare as humanity facing a new Goliath, a vision of derelict religion and a world without God. His stare was calm and sober and unflinching.

We walked to the south bank of the Arno, past the old city gate into the spacious Piazzale Michelangelo to watch a glorious sunset and the lights winking on throughout the busy metropolis as domes and towers became purple silhouettes at dusk. The buildings of Florence are what I call brick Gothic, a product of a new style in architecture and incredible civic zeal. Most of those towers and domes rising above the streets are the legacy of the powerful Medici family. The Uffizi was their administrative offices, the cathedral and Duomo the pet project of the founder, Cosomo Medici, and the vast Pallaza Pitti was their private palace.

I liked especially the Duomo, and in fact on the plane ride to Italy I read a book about its architect, Brunelleschi's Dome by Ross King. Brunelleschi was an archetypal "Renaissance man," a combination artist, engineer and inventor. One of his inventions, a reverse gear for an ox-powered crane to lift the 70,000 tons of brick and marble for the dome, used to be attributed to Leonardo da Vinci because Leonardo hand copied some of the designs in order to learn mechanics. Brunelleschi began the construction of the Duomo at a time when technology did not exist to complete the structure. He invented techniques to build arches without central scaffolding, and in the process reinvented architecture. He invented techniques to build at 270 feet above the cathedral floor and so create the world's largest dome.

King's book is filled with stories of the political intrigues and engineering marvels surrounding the 20-year construction effort, and it teems with details of the arts in 15th Century Florence. I learned, for example, that Brunelleschi had to establish special safety measures for the construction site. He forbade masons working on high to have wine at lunch that was not diluted with water. He prohibited masons on platforms hanging from the roof from swinging across the yawning abyss to catch the pigeons that roosted in crevices opposite. Also, the author explains how, in the days before anyone understood electricity, the people used to place carcasses of eagles in the belfries in order to ward off lightning.

In preparation for the trip I also read a book about the government of Italy, or the city states that made up Italy at the onset of the Renaissance. Florence in the 15th Century was theoretically a republic but actually an oligarchy run by the Medici family. In Medici Money by Tim Parks I learned where the Medici family got its money and how they used it to promote the arts (and the wars and the Medici). I suspected that understanding the Renaissance meant appreciating the wherewithal for social change – the affluence, the concentration of power, in short: the money.

A friend had suggested that the explanation for any renaissance was a simple mechanism: affluence produces leisure which produces art. Maybe so, or at least money may be a vital part of the story. I tend to play down that aspect of culture in my own mind because I was brought up in a working class American family where great wealth was scorned, or at least distrusted. My parents grew up in the Depression Era, and so they developed a cynicism about the rich and privileged class whose greed they thought caused, or aggravated, the collapse of the economy. As a dyed-in-the-wool American, I also imbibed with my mother's milk a scorn for European style aristocracy and the notion of monarchy and a privileged class. But I may have short-changed the importance of wealth. I am beginning to see that lots of money, possessed for lots of years, tends to go hand-in-hand with patronage and the efflorescence of the arts.

Some historians correlate the Renaissance with a decline in the influence of a corrupt Roman Church and a subsequent rise in humanism. This is a powerful idea but largely, I suspect, a fiction invented by historians. It seems unlikely that people reasoned that "the Church has failed us, so let's become more human." Tim Parks calls this thinking an outrage: "...what makes most of us humanists in fact, is the movement's greatest outrage: its dismissal of what came before as a thousand years of darkness, as if the middle ages had somehow been *inhuman*."

The Medici founded the most powerful institution of the Middle Ages (after the Church), the international bank. They funded wool merchants of Florence and alum miners in Turkey and ship captains in England. They also funded much of the constant warfare that plagued the late Middle Ages. For two or three generations in the 15th Century, the seaport of Venice attacked the trading center at Milan, which in turn invaded the wool industry at Florence, which besieged the port of Genoa. Engineers like Leonardo and Brunelleschi supplemented their artistic work by designing fortifications and weapons. And behind it all, the corrupt Catholic Church at Rome (this was before Savonarola and Luther began their reforms) plotted and finagled and aided and abetted the mayhem. Many historians suggest that patronage of the arts was a form of penance, that the worldly Medici financed frescoes in cathedrals and statuary in chapels as a means to expiate sin. They wanted to buy their way into heaven. The motto of the Medici bank, engraved above the counting house door, was "For God and for profit."

The forces that led to the Renaissance, then, included not just money but also political struggle, warfare, and a declining Church. Ellen thinks that disgust with the Church may be the key – a centuries old social oppression, from the Church (or pharoah's tax collectors or whatever), and then a burst of freedom. Renaissance, she thinks, is the release of creative juices following a period of oppression, something like popping the cork on good champagne.

25

At the end of the wonderful film noir called <u>The Third Man</u>, the character played by Orson Welles says "Italy had thirty years of constant warfare, treachery and bloodshed, and they produced Michelangelo, Leonardo and the Renaissance. Switzerland had 500 years of peace and democracy and they produced – the cuckoo clock!"

Tuscany

We had intended to stay several days in Florence, but the fine weather and autumn foliage beckoned, so we broke camp and headed for the hills of Tuscany (or, as they say, Toscana, or as they used to say, Etruscan land). The road wound through verdant valleys dotted with olive groves. We chugged up hills and roared down vales. Oddly, considering the abundance of local cheeses, Parmesan and Gorgonzolla and the like, we saw no goats and almost no cattle in all of Tuscany. About the only animal life we saw in Italy was cats – cats in piazzas, cats on balconies, cats in alleys and cats in store windows. Cats seem to gather around Ellen like moths to a flame. One suspects witchcraft.

At the end of one valley we parked and climbed a small mountain to enter San Gimignano, a village famed for twelve soaring towers (12 remaining of 72 built at the zenith of civic egotism). The towers pop up from the village proud and erect like 80-foot high phallic symbols. We stopped at a charming inn outside Sienna to taste a regional specialty, white beans cooked in a Chianti container.

As the sunset streamed gold on the highway, we began to meander around looking for a hotel, but we got lost (of course) and darkness fell. We criss-crossed the tollway and village lanes in growing frustration until we took a winding gravel road deep into the countryside to discover, hallelujah, a charming villa with extensive grounds just outside the village of Castellena en Chianti. I asked the innkeeper what it cost, and he named a fair price. I leaped at it because I was exhausted and desperate. He could have asked for the car keys and my pants.

Morning sunlight poured upon the terraces of Villa Casalecchi. Presumably the place had been the mansion of a family called Lecchi (or perhaps a family from Lecce). At breakfast the view from the terrace was olive trees and an attached vineyard that ran down the valley and halfway up the distant hills. The villa sported a cerulean blue swimming pool set in terra-cotta tiles. Below our terrace stood a quiet rose garden and a persimmon tree laden with yellow-orange fruit.

We extended our stay at the villa by *una notte* and set off for more Tuscany. More green and golden hills, winding country roads and on all sides the vineyards of Chianti. The flora of Tuscany and the trees especially reminded me of the landscape backgrounds in Leonardo's paintings, with hilltop silhouettes of fan-shaped pines and spire-like junipers.

We explored a tiny perched village called Montereggio that had preserved its medieval character, with a small church and graveyard, a few shops and a public fountain enclosed in high stone walls atop a steep hill. The economics of such a small place, 150 residents in the 13th Century according to archeologists, made it more impressive. Imagine an American farm village of 150 people mustering the money and the will to encircle the town with a 30-foot high stone wall, and imagine the audacity of 150 townspeople defying the attacks and sieges of raiding armies from Sienna – or, for that matter, Florence, Milan and France. Imagine the great labor involved in hauling tons of hand-cut rock up that hillside to enclose a marketplace, a small jewel box church and a community well. It speaks to the perils of the times and also to the sense of timelessness for the villagers. They could devote years or decades or multiple generations to build a fortress to defend a few vineyards and olive groves because the father and son and grandson alike spent their lives in a landscape of unchanging eternity.

Tower at Sienna

At Sienna the huge brick-paved Piazza del Campo swarmed with tourists and sun bathers. No one seemed in much of a hurry, the Italians being seriously dedicated to *la dolce far niete*. Under a medieval fountain of a marble dog spouting a stream of water, the pigeons vied for turns at the shower. We browsed the souvenir stands. Our wardrobes had been depleted because of the warm weather – we had packed for a rainy fall and got a balmy Indian summer – so Ellen got a

28

t-shirt with Coca-Cola sign lettering that said "Ciao, Bella!" and I got a t-shirt of Leonardo's naked man circumscribed.

More walking and yet more walking the winding narrow streets which Ellen said reminded her of Venice, without the water. Sienna, like Padua, is an ancient university town. We stopped at a student-run café where I had a semi-circular sandwich like a pizza and Ellen got a whole wheat roll loaded with sardine paste. I liked the fact that I could spot the students by now, the scruffy young people in black t-shirts and unkempt hair, wandering Sienna like a zombie army.

We came at last to the cathedral of Santa Maria de la Scala (Our Lady of the Ladder?), and despite disappointment to find the ornate front covered with scaffolding (which was swathed in a plastic film printed with an image of the cathedral façade), we were awed by the cathedral interior, the high late medieval ceiling of lapis lazuli blue and beaten gold and the pale blue stained glass windows. The floor shone with intricate mosaics in red and white marble of knights on chargers and ladies on lutes. The side chapels held huge illuminated medieval hymn books with square music notes. Frescoes by Donatello and others on the library walls showed lively Tuscan crowds where each guild and class was distinguished by an odd-shaped hat.

Under the main cathedral we found a "crypt" which was actually a waiting room of the original medieval church. It was installed and painted in 1278, then abandoned, buried in rubble and forgotten for 700 years. In 1996 the room was unearthed and turned into a museum. Vibrantly colored frescoes nearly as fresh as the day they were painted adorn the walls. The frescoes told Old Testament and New Testament stories to the illiterate pilgrims waiting to enter the glory of the Sienna cathedral. I realized that I too was such a pilgrim, only shorn of medieval reverence and 700 years late for the service.

Another mountain climb back to the parking lot and then a half-hour drive to the villa for a hot bath and nap. We had drinks on the terrace. The barmaid had never heard of a martini, even though they had all the fixings including probably locally grown olives. I had to show her how to mix the gin and vermouth and ice to produce a frosty one stirred but not shaken. The sun sank behind the vineyard and hills, and we talked until the swallows gliding overhead disappeared in the dark and then reappeared as bats. Then we drove off to town to discover a pizzeria that featured a buffet spread, like Italian smorgasbord. After *cappucino* I tried to tip the staff for the excellent meal, but they shook their heads "no." Per usual, the tip is included in the "service charge" that is added to every bill to cover delivery of bread and olive oil and attention.

Pisa

Reluctantly we ended our pleasant interlude at the villa and drove west to the mouth of the Arno River at Pisa. Once Pisa was a bustling seaport of the Roman empire. Once Pisa rivaled Venice and Genoa as a place to unload shipments of wool and iron and to take on cargoes of pottery and cloth. Once the rare white marble from the northern quarry at Carrara was floated down the coast of the Ligurian Sea to Pisa, then transferred to barges and floated east on the shallow Arno to Florence, where it was sliced and carved and polished to build the great Duomo of Bruneschelli and the haunting statues of Michelangelo.

Once Pisa was all commerce, but today it seems less like a port than a modest suburb, surviving on a lively tourist trade that stems from a certain civic boo-boo. The last time I visited Pisa, no one was allowed to enter the tower because it was sinking and tilting worse (or better) than ever. The Leaning Tower of Pisa ten years ago was anchored to giant cement blocks and held in place by giant steel bands. This time tourists were allowed to climb the 360 steps of spiral stairway to the top.

I recommend the climb if only for the fun-house effects of leaning far forward to pound up a set of stairs, turn the corner, and then lean over backwards to mount the next steps. At the summit one beholds a fine view of the city and also a set of eight massive bronze bells. The Leaning Tower, besides being a physics lab for Galileo, was also a campanile. I got my picture taken trying to mount footholds of one giant bell in order to swing out over the city and clang the bell like Quasimodo.

After the tower climb I found a shop and bought cones of luscious gelato in strawberry, banana, lemon and pear. Next, we visited the Camposanto opposite the Leaning Tower. I recommend the walk because the huge cemetery complex contains impressive statuary for the dead who were displaced from the old graveyard to make way for the cathedral. By sheer luck I found a grave and statue dedicated to one of my minor heroes, the mathematician (and presumably resident of Pisa) Fibonacci. At the back of the cemetery lurks a cavernous room decorated with medieval frescoes that borrow heavily from Dante's vision of Paradise and the Inferno. Medieval ladies in veils and knights on horseback stand at the threshold of the afterlife; in one direction lie gardens and purling streams, and in the other direction bristle fire and brimstone and tortured sinners being prodded by demons. The devil looks like a man-gobbling monster from an early episode of Dr. Who.

Portofino

From Pisa we drove northwest on the tollway, plunging through tunnels that brought alternate bursts of blazing sunshine and shadows of the mountain bowels, until we began to encounter the Italian Riviera. Picturesque villages of parchment-colored stucco homes with terra-cotta roofs clung to steep hillsides that plunged down to an azure sea. Palm trees sprouted from street corners and bougainvillea tumbled from balconies. It felt like Nice or Antibes or

Monte Carlo. We stopped at one such village, Portofino, with hotels clumped on steep mountain sides and a quiet marina dotted with Goldfinger yachts. Our hotel was built into the mountain side and so, after unloading, we drove around a steep bend into the village to park in a city lot. From our balcony we could just glimpse the steep path threading down to the private beach.

We hiked over yet another mountain into the village for a dockside dinner of seafood fettuccini and a bottle of mellow Soave. The specialty cuisine of the Ligurian region, invented in Genoa or thereabouts, is pesto. Here the basil and garlic sauce was served on spiral fusilli with diced potato.

Sunday morning we went for a swim in the little cove below the Piccolo Hotel. The Ligurian Sea was brisk but not chilly, very clear and bouncing with one-foot swells. The shoreline was covered with marble pebbles and what Ellen called "sea glass" – rounded chips of glass, water-worn, azure and bottle green and Prussian blue.

We headed back over our route of the previous evening, this time motoring southeast through the seaside mountain range to visit the region known as Cinque Terre, named for five villages lining the Ligurian coast. When I had checked out of the gracious Piccolo Hotel, the clerk asked where we were going, and when I replied Cinque Terre [cheenk-hu ted-uh], and he asked for how long. I said, momentarily confused, that we would stay there two days [*due giorni*, doo-eh jorn-ee]. He sighed and said, "Two days in Cinque Terre… and only one in Portofino." He shook his head in sorrow and wonder.

Snow sheets peeped from mountain tops as we drove along, and a pewter sea glittered far below. We intended to hike along the high mountain trail that links the Cinque Terre fishing villages. We parked at roadside on a precipitous cliff and headed down yet another mountain, but the pavement was slippery with mist, the village choked with tourists, our parking spot vaguely illegal and rain clouds gathering far out at sea. We turned back and rescued the forlorn rental car hanging in space. Light rain spattered the windshield and I congratulated myself on dodging the showers, but when I crossed the mountain range again, I realized that the threat of rain was merely a coastal phenomenon. The eastern side of the mountains baked in steady golden sunlight. The main memory I have of Cinque Terre, then, is a story from the guidebook. It explains that the villages of that remote coast were connected by a trail called the Via d'Amore because would-be lovers walked the trail in hopes of finding a spouse in a distant village, outside their village's limited gene pool.

Italian Lake Region

After a quick reconnoiter we decided to skip lunch, skip the museums of Genoa (sorry 'bout that, Columbus!) and head past Milan into the Lake Region of northern Italy. This is where Italy begins to veer into Switzerland, the area famed for glacier-fed lakes and posh resorts like Lake Como. While studying the map I discovered a place southeast of Milan called Busetto, the home town of the opera giant,

Giuseppi Verdi (Joe Green). Ellen leaped at the idea of visiting the fellow's home town and possibly catching a performance at the tiny Verdi Teatro. So we left the tollway and got lost two or twelve times on bumpy one-horse rural roads and asked directions in a biker bar and finally, in the dark, stumbled upon the private estate of the composer, the Villa Verdi, just outside Busetto.

The place was nothing much, just a stucco mansion within a nice walled garden in a non-descript town of rural Lombardy. It might have been interesting in daylight, but it was just a looming curiosity behind barred gates at night. We drove into the village and came upon a square with a flood-lit statue of Verdi seated at his writing desk. The cozy tourist office informed us that nothing was playing at that time in Verdi Teatro, but come back in three weeks. We were ravenous, so we got probably the most authentic Italian meal of the trip at a small-town café, The fixed price meal consisted of seven kinds of lard. We had fatty salami accompanied by slices of ham laced with glistening seams of fat, pickled vegetables, a kind of greasy bread, tangy chunks of parmesan cheese (we were only 30 km from Parma), and for *dolce* some sort of fried cookie. Cholesterol count somewhere in the zillions. I ordered a half carafe of the house red wine (*vino rosso della casa, per favore*), placing my faith in the mythical medicinal virtues of red wine.

Italian deli

We drove into the night, past Milan and the airport exit, and before we knew it, we hit the southern side of Como. I grew weary of motel searching along the tollway, so we took the next exit and wheeled around several village streets until we encountered a group of gray-haired Italian men, pretty obviously well-oiled and resembling a mobile Shriner convention. In jocular pidgin Italian and English they directed us to a motel, the only one in town, and by a small miracle we found it and got a room. At the motel bar we chatted about causes of the Renaissance and the forces of war, church and money, but all I remember is weary gratitude for the anesthetic properties of gin.

Lake Como looks just like the postcards – an expansive blue-water lake surrounded by Alpine foothills. We hiked down yet another vertical path to investigate a chalet that turned out to be a boat house, closed for the season. Neatly stacked kayaks. A big water spray just offshore made a fan-shaped rainbow. A funicular, I think, climbed the hills across the lake.

We drove up to Bellagio, a village at the tip of a peninsula projecting between the finger lakes of the area. The drive to Bellagio is an alarming series of hairpin curves on a very narrow mountain road, but the place is worth the effort. We parked at the shore and wandered into the spectacular grounds of the Villa Malzi. At the entrance we found a grotto and a footpath around a reflecting pool lined with tangerine-colored Japanese maples. Huge old North American cypress and tulip trees cast shadows on the flower beds, and a sycamore-lined path led to the villa itself, a regal mansion with gables and stables and a veranda overlooking the calm waters of the lake. One of the outbuildings had been converted to a museum of Etruscan and Greek statuary. The boat house with sky-blue cupola was lined with portraits of the nobles, mostly appointed by Napoleon III, who peopled the villa in the 19th Century. The site was a public garden now (but still privately owned), a place so achingly lovely as to seem unreal, like the Baron's estate in <u>The Sound of Music</u>.

Despite its hoity-toity reputation and the gaudy spectacle of its Las Vegas namesake, Bellagio turned out to be a pleasant and relaxed tourist town. Ferries across Lake Como arrived at the dock every half hour or so, disgorging a stream of tourists intent on shopping and gelato. Kids played in the shade of lakeside pines. Locals sat in the piazza and soaked up late fall sunshine. We had a modest spaghetti lunch at a café beside the ferry landing, followed by a delicious sundae *capa Montecarlo* with orange liqueur and caramel dribbles and a rolled biscotti on top, like an elegant dreamsicle.

We opted to drive back to Como in daylight, a life-saving measure considering the challenges of the mountain roads. That evening we strolled the lake front and stopped at a supermarket behind an ornate Romanesque cathedral ghostly in streetlights, like a castle dipped in white chocolate. For souvenirs we bought pesto and balsamic vinegar. Footsore we returned to our Best Western Hotel and watched an in-room movie, the new version of <u>Pride and Prejudice</u>, a blatant, egregious, over the top romance. I guess I was getting weary of all the romantic *fol-de-rol* in Italy, and a dose of Jane Austen was more than I could stand. I recalled that Mark Twain had the right idea. Twain said, "If a person had a library that contained none of the works of Jane Austen, then, even if it had no other books, it would still be a pretty good library."

Italian Renaissance

On the plane ride home I got to thinking about the gorgeous garden and the villa in Bellagio. Here was another instance of accumulated wealth resulting in the creation of lasting beauty. Not a Renaissance, of course, but still an example of what money and leisure and taste can accomplish.

The portraits of the aristocrats in the villa haunted me. I thought of all those dainty belles with empress waistlines and hair piled up in tight curls, all those sharp-chinned lords in epaulets and fashion swords. I imagined their horse rides through olive groves, their waltzes on the veranda, their pleasure boating on the lake. These nobles were a puppet aristocracy, of course, set up by Napoleon after he whupped the Austrians and chased the Pope from Rome in 1804. Their courtier life was genteel, and transient and phony as a cardboard crown.

I won't bore you with the history of Italy (see next travelogue for boring history of France), since it is as messy, colorful and confusing as the street signs of Venice. It suffices to say that while the Renaissance came early to Italy, nationalism came late. The Italians have always been too busy cutting each other's throats to bother much with constitutional law. They wrangled their way through the 19th Century and instituted the merry-go-round form of government, culminating in the pathetic Fascist state which our fathers spanked. Since the collapse of Rome, Italy has been less a nation than a free-for-all, and Napoleon's Bourbon monarchy was just another wayward joke.

I thought that probably the departure of the Bourbons was good riddance, and yet, undeniably, in their wake they left Italy and us tourista something to ponder, something graceful and elegant. Maybe it was the romance of Italy that stole into my thoughts, or maybe just world-weary resignation, but something tender arose from imagining all the lords and ladies who pursued civilization in the midst of chaos. They sipped their champagne and pruned their gardens and soon passed into memory. By the time the cypress trees matured, their exclusive playground had become a public park. Their empire was just a dream from which we the people are trying to awake. The same may be said for the Caesars and the Medici and the Bourbons, that their power and glory inevitably fade away. We the people inherit the beauty. *Ciao, bella.*

France

Normandy

If liberty is dear to you, may you never discover that my face is love's prison.
-- Leonardo Davinci

The opportunity to take a summer vacation came up at the last minute, and Ellen had not yet swept into my life, so I burned 100,000 frequent flyer miles to get a flight to Paris. Since I wanted the freedom of a driving vacation, I booked a modest rental car at Charles De Gaulle (CDG) airport, mindful that, for European roads, smaller is better. Then I sat down with an old map and drew a big yellow loop representing a driving tour of Normandy, Brittany and the Loire Valley. Based on hints from a guidebook to France I selected some interesting sights and villages near those sites, and then I used Google and Travelocity to book eight hotel rooms in seven different villages. The next day I located my passport, packed some clean underwear and flew to Paris. The amazing thing is that it worked. You can do it too, if you have a few hours (okay, several hours) for Internet research, and the confidence of ignorance.

The trip started off on the wrong foot because a malfunction in the jetliner windshield washer delayed takeoff for four hours. My driving timetable was shot to pieces. Arriving sleepless and ragged mid-day at CDG, I bought a better map of France and discovered that I landed at the wrong airport. CDG was northeast of Paris and my first destination was northwest, so I had to navigate around the big city. It didn't help that, annoyingly, all the traffic signs were in French.

Giverny

Eventually my trusty Vauxhall Meriva, a compact sedan advertised to seat four adults (if they are koalas) threaded its way around Paris and zoomed along country roads past rolling fields, 300-year-old stone farmhouses, and assorted churches, cafes and gas stations to the rural village of Giverny.

Giverny hosts the country estate of the artist Claude Monet. It includes his home and studio plus large surrounding gardens, the subject matter of some of his best-loved paintings and pastels. The entrance gave onto the American Garden, a donation from the American philanthropist Terra (lately of Chicago). The first picture I snapped was a meadow studded with bright red-orange poppies. Like getting a postcard from Renoir.

The Monet Garden was magnificent. Even though thronged with tourists, it opened onto a quiet, meditative space, with graceful walkways among sculpted trees, long rows of colorful roses, and at the back his famous lily ponds, splendid with hundreds of vermillion lily/lotus/nymphae blooms and graceful Japanese bridges. Monet's Maison, a spacious two-story stone chalet, was preserved with his original color scheme – one-bedroom blue and one white, the kitchen Prussian blue with Dresden tiles and a stunning sunflower-yellow dining room. The walls were hung with a treasury of Japanese prints including a score of superb landscapes by Hiroshige Uttagawa. The best room was a large reception space at the entrance. An old black-and-white photo showed Monet standing in that exact room, surrounded by the same 3-piece sofa, chaise lounge, wicker desk and chairs, and backlit by the huge north light window. In the photo Monet is nestled among his paintings, but today the walls are hung with reproductions. [Later in the trip I was to see many of those originals displayed in Paris at the Musee d'Orsay.] The profusion of paintings at the entrance made Monet's place bright, welcoming and a little overwhelming. An onslaught of art.

Leaving the Monet Foundation grounds I passed a half-trailer set up as a vending stand for home-made ice cream. I ordered a small pistachio cone (*une petite cornette pistache, s'il vous plais*) that contained no pistachios but plenty of fragrant almond extract, and snarfed it down before it could melt.

Bayeaux

Next I drove directly for the Normandy coast, skipping the huge Abbaye of Caen (sorry to miss you, Caen!) and the Cathedral of Rouen where they burned Joan of Arc (sorry 'bout that, Rouen!). The flight delay had put me four hours late in getting to my motel in Bayeaux. I had no energy for the hoary glories of Caen and Rouen; just a pooped tourist who needed some sleep.

Slept twelve hours solid. The motel breakfast was unremarkable -- so naturally I will remark on it. I tried a packaged foodstuff labeled "Compote de Pommes" which turned out to be plain applesauce. The big bowl of chopped fruit contained apples, oranges, grapes and, oddly, diced tomatoes. Not bad.

The parking lot of my ultramodern Novotel was filled with wheelchairs and long, low-to-the-ground racing cycles, like go-karts with pedals mounted up where the handlebars would go. Paraplegics and well-wishers had gathered in the parking lot to sign up for some sort of race – and of course to covet each other's nifty cycles. Later in the day I was to pass billboards announcing the all-France Championship for *Cyclisme Handisport*. By watching the participants take a few practice laps around the nearby traffic circle, I think I picked out the likely winner – a guy with no legs (less weight) and forearms like Popeye.

The plan for my first full day in Normandy was to visit the beaches where the Allies made the D-Day landing. At the outskirts of Bayeaux I found the Musee de Bataille Normandie, but it was closed for repairs. A nice female ensign in uniform directed me to a temporary alternative, a trailer parked beside the museum packed with photos to display the good life in today's French Navy: helicopter rides, exotic shore leave and scuba diving. The French sea chantries on the loudspeakers and the guys in fins made me think of Jacques Cousteau.

Normandy Beachhead

The way out of Bayeaux to the coast was blocked – naturally – by hand-driven bicycle races. I took a detour (and you would think the French word for Detour is "detour", but no, out of sheer perversity the French road sign declared a *Deviation*). Wound up in a soldiers' cemetery. Big grassy space decorated with flags and pale marble statues. Narrow gravel paths between sections of graves. In all directions stretched long rows of stark white gravestones. The air held an intense silence except for a lanyard banging against a flagpole and the distant cars hissing on asphalt. Approaching an individual gravestone, I discovered that it was the British section of the honored dead. In this particular grave lay Rifleman C. Woodcraft of Dorsetshire, aged 20. I imagined a kid with glasses and British buck teeth and overlarge ears and a mop of chestnut hair. Stepping back from that very individual marker caused it to blend immediately into the mass of identical headstones. Rifleman Woodcraft vanished in the vast anonymity of the dead.

Suddenly, I know where Jimmy Hoffa is buried: Arlington National Cemetery.

The twenty of so kilometers between Bayeaux and the coast is mostly rolling hills and farmland. In fact, most of Normandy might be Wisconsin, except for the 300-year-old stone houses and barns and silos. Large cylinders of harvested hay bulge above healthy green fields. Scattered stands of maples and chestnuts and birch. Smell of manure in the air. Small signs at roadside promoting campgrounds and little motels (*chambers toutes conforts*), and smatterings of tiny white wildflowers and blue cornflowers and red poppies.

Omaha Beach is quiet now. Just past the parking lot you take a sand path among clumps of sea grass. Walking silently over a dune, you emerge on a stretch of tan sand and glittering sea. The tide is out at noon and yet you hear from fifty meters away the hushed wash of the sea. It is perfectly quiet and serene now, except for scattered cries of seagulls and distant cries of children playing at sand castles.

And you try to imagine how it was on D-Day, the ground pulsing from artillery shell impact, the stink of gunpowder, the cumulative roar from battleship guns and airplanes droning overhead and machinegun fire and the screams of young men dying. On that first day, June 6, 1944, on that stretch of beach alone, three thousand eight hundred thirty-one soldiers died, more in the first hour than in all the years of war with Iraq.

Back from the beach on a rise, an old German blockhouse still keeps watch. The nose of an anti-aircraft gun protrudes from a slit in the concrete block. Inside the blockhouse, in cool shade, the gun appears badly rusted, but it still sweeps a wide swath of beach. A plaque outside states that naval guns blasted this particular blockhouse and allowed the 1st Infantry Brigade (Big Red One) to take the position and establish the first road to the interior of France. The village of Bayeaux was the first large town liberated.

Further down the beach a bride steps out of the sunlight, dressed in white satin and taffeta veils. The groom in a black tuxedo poses beside her, and a photographer snaps their wedding pictures, just there, in the waves where sixty years ago bobbed a hundred torn corpses.

Driving back to the interior from the old battleground, I felt like I could use a drink. The Normandy region of France is famous for its apples, and in fact many of the bakeries, *boulangeries,* offer apple tarts as *tartes Normande.* Common along the road stand small apple orchards which advertise Calvados, the local apple brandy. I turned onto a dirt road that led to an ancient stone farmhouse with an enclosed porch and shelves of dusty green bottles. The proprietor spoke little English and so we danced a tiny lingual minuet before we found enough pidgin for me to ask for a drink. His place was small (10 hectares) and he bottled all his own wares. I tasted his apple juice (*jus de pommes*) and cider (*cidre* – 5% alcohol) and Calvados (40% alcohol). The brandy was warm but not fragrant, and besides I had driving to do, so I drank a glass of the *cidre* fizzing like flavored champagne, and struck a deal for a couple of bottles. The proprietor prolonged my visit by insisting on giving me a brief tour of the orchard, bee hives, fermentation vats and chicken coop. I think he enjoyed my visit because I my American accent made me talk funny.

Bayeaux Tapestry

I drove back to Bayeaux (BAH-you, *mon vieux*) to see the famous tapestry. It's an odd coincidence – or maybe not a coincidence at all – to come from the beach where the Allies invaded France from the North and then head directly to view a tapestry that celebrates the invasion of England from the South. The village of Bayeaux is directly across the English Channel (*La Manche*) from Portsmouth, the notable harbor town in England.

The Bayeaux Tapestry is just a piece of linen cloth adorned with colored woolen thread. The fact that such fragile stuff has survived 900 years is a minor miracle. It is huge, 70 meters long, and the museum where it is housed contains an annotated facsimile of the tapestry, plus a movie about its contents, plus a winding corridor of glass cases containing the document itself.

The tapestry provides a unique historical record because it is actually a giant cartoon that tells the story behind the Norman invasion of England. I won't bore you with all the historical details (I'll do that later), but the outline of the tale is simple enough: treacherous Harold of England seized the throne upon the death of King Edward the Confessor, even though he had sworn to honor the claim to the throne of Guilliame of Normandy (known as William the Bastard and later as William the Conqueror). This peeved William, and so he chopped down a forest and built a hundred ships and invaded England and routed the Saxons. All this carnage occurred in 1066, and the British islanders have been miffed about it ever since.

I learned in the museum bookstore that the Normans were actually Danes or Norwegians, Viking stock, who had invaded northern France only 200 years earlier. Back in those days the Danes were not much different from the English who were not that different from the French. They were all tribes where big louts with clubs and swords ganged up on the local shepherds and stole their livestock and women and then built rock castles and drank all the wine. My, how times have changed.

The Bayeaux Tapestry is both crude and sophisticated – crude because the medium, stitches of thread, limits representative detail and so the English characters are indicated by the fact that they have mustaches – and sophisticated because keen psychological insight permeates the story, like the detail that wicked Harold was touching sacred relics when he swore fealty to William and therefore his offense was both to honor and to God. The edges of the tapestry sport griffins, sea serpents, animals from Aesop's fables and a cornucopia of irrelevant but fascinating details on medieval life. The main scenes contain ingenious art work like the streaming arrows and severed heads at the Battle of Hastings and the ominous appearance of Halley's Comet just before the invasion. The tapestry delights in homely detail, like the carpenters rushing to complete the invasion fleet and the army stocking the ships with sheep, pigs, armament and of course kegs of wine. There must be a hundred books and a thousand French doctoral dissertations on the throwaway detail of the tapestry. It is more than a story in graphic art form. It is history made tangible.

Barfleur

From Bayeaux I headed west into the Cotentin Peninsula to catch a glimpse of a Normandy fishing village. I missed my exit and barged into Cherbourg. I hesitated to navigate yet another city center (*centre ville*) thick with pedestrians, and so I bypassed Cherbourg, but not without regret. The mental image of a young Catherine Deneuve in the musical "Umbrellas of Cherbourg" is enough to make you forget to breathe.

Driving along the rim of the peninsula presents stunning views of La Manche and craggy limestone cliffs plunging down into sparkling grey-blue water. I stopped to snap photos of hollyhocks on a cliff path. The area reminds me of more Wisconsin, only this time a large and rugged Door County. Briefly I stopped outside Cherbourg harbor to tour a promontory overlooking the shipping channels, Fort Cap de Levi. As I fumbled to read the plaque of posted tourist information, I gradually realized that "cap" means "cape" and that the French word for "fort" is – duh – "fort".

Barfleur, according to my guide book (Eyewitness Travel Guides: France by Dorling Kindersley), is a fishing village, and indeed the wharf was strewn with fishing nets. But if it is a working fishing village, they don't work very hard. None of the fishing boats in the marina was manned, and the nets were clogged with old oyster shells. I meandered by the old church and discovered down below in the tide pools rocks covered with countless snail and limpet shells. Drank a Stella at a dockside café preparatory to dinner but found the smell of the seafood mingled with the stench of the docks overwhelming.

Headed back to Bayeaux to spend a second night, passing through thick forest. More Wisconsin. Passed a village east of St Pierre Eglise called Tocqueville and wondered if that was the home of the historian. Now very proud of myself because I stopped at an *auberge* (county inn) outside La Forge d'Yvelot and ordered dinner, joked with a pretty waitress and tipped appropriately -- all without speaking a word of English. I had a *brochette campagnale* (kabob with annouille sausage, apples, onions, tomato) plus *frites* (fries) and a half bottle of the local Saumur Champigny Rouge. The salad tasted fresh, just picked, and the sausage had a wild pork flavor with thick skin and the *crème brulee* was perfect. The sun was just setting at 10 p.m. when I left, and I noticed that none of the French patrons left before me. These French take their food seriously. They take one-and-a-half to two hours minimal per meal, and they order extra courses like a wine appetizer, mussels (*moules*) before the entrée and salad before the dessert. There appears to be no French phrase for "fast food".

On the return to Bayeaux I stopped to pee in the bushes and watched a dozen bats flit among the darkened trees.

Sunday I planned to drive to Mont St. Michel with stops in St Lo and Avranches. More Wisconsin scenery, including farm machinery lumbering on back roads, a hay wagon loaded precariously, and herds of spotted cows – not the black-and-white breed you see in Wisconsin, but spotted chalk white and milk chocolate brown, with goofy friendly patches on their faces. That is another parallel with Wisconsin, exceptionally fine cheese country. In rural France, between the entree and dessert they serve a plate of Camembert fit to tickle the nostrils of the gods. I found it easier to find good cheese in France than to find a brick in Philadelphia. The variety can be overwhelming. Charles DeGaulle, when trying to build a ruling coalition in post-war France remarked, "How can anyone govern a nation that has two hundred and forty-six different kinds of cheese?"

Coutances Cathedral

En route to the seashore, I stopped in Coutances to see a fine gothic cathedral. There was no mass at the museum/cathedral but a ceremony was being held on the grounds, complete with flags and trumpets and long speeches in memory of *les enfants Coutances qui a mort pour France.* At the end of the speeches the church bells erupted in raucous peals. I took my customary morning meal, croissant and café au lait, at a nearby café and then wandered into the public gardens. Oddly the bushes and plots of luxuriant ground cover were decorated with cut-outs of saxophones. In the center of the garden a flower bed was planted with the motto: *Jazz Sous Les Panniers.* The phrase means, I think, "jazz under the palms" – but it could be "jazz under the pantaloons."

My next stop was Granville, an old port and tourist town. From the high tower above the port, Le Roc, one can see across La Manche the dim outline of England. I skipped the mundane tourist attractions around the harbor in favor of hiking up to Haute Ville, the old village high above the busy port and site of a modern orange-painted lighthouse with a beautiful view of the azure shallows far below. Down on the beach I spotted swimmers in the surf and a group of men launching a blue rubber raft and a covey of women sunning themselves on blankets. Granville is that rarity on the cold Atlantic coast that offers shallow water beaches warm enough for swimming. It occurred to me that mine is the first American generation to live, start to finish, in the Age of the Bikini. Hallelujah, praise the Lord!

The day was too fine for driving, so I lolled on the terrace of the restaurant "L'Echauguette" in Haute Ville. Ordered *crepe gratiniere coquille St Jacques* (a pancake stuffed with tiny sweet scallops, covered with Gruyere cheese and baked). Following the lead of a woman at the next table – I just ordered *le meme de madame* – dessert arrived as another crepe and a waiter carrying a pan of Grand Marnier (yellow label) and a small blowtorch. He heated the brandy and then poured it flaming atop my crepe. I asked if that was *crepe suzette*, but he said no – and the bill later confirmed it – as *crepe natural*.

On the way down the hill I stopped at the Aquarium, an attraction which normally I would skip, except that my guide book said it contained *La Feerie de Coquillage* (Seashell Wonderland). It proved to be what I hoped – the quirkiest museum in the land. The first part was an amazing insect and butterfly collection with thousands of specimens displayed in glass-faced boxes. There were foot-long walking sticks and frozen tarantula and horned beetles the size of softballs. The Lepidoptera made a kaleidoscope of gleaming colors, scarlet and spotted yellow and iridescent blue, all arranged by geographic habitat. Vladimir Nabokov

57

would have swooned to see such a manifestation of beauty and death.

The next part was a mundane path through murky fish tanks, but that was followed quickly by a strange rock collection. The usual chunks of agate and opal and wotnot led to rooms full of rock-enhanced sculpture – life-sized roosters and dragons and monkeys and cats encrusted with amethyst and garnet and tigers-eye. And that led to rooms of seashell creations. There was a Taj Mahal made of scallop shells and a life-sized mermaid of 10,000 shells and pearls and a group of dolls in lacey Victorian dress composed entirely of seashells and mosaics and sculpture and a fountain made of giant clam shells. It was a seashell extravaganza, an homage to fetishism, a temple of the bizarre leading to the sublime.

Driving west again and nearly in Brittany I stopped at Avranches where my guide book promised a fine view of Mont St. Michel. None of the signage pointed me to the viewing site, the Jardin Avranches, so I drove toward the highest spire in town and sure enough, that took me to the cathedral which took me to the crest of the old town which took me to the public gardens. The view, however, was disappointing. Mont St. Michel was just a dim blip on the horizon, at the end of a serpentine river that led to the sea.

Walking back to the car I paused to watch a flock of French school children cross the street. They were dressed as frogs. Really. This was a Sunday afternoon and yet here was a string of 30-40 kids aged six to eight giggling and whooping as they straggled behind their teachers. All were wearing green construction paper headdress with bumps at the top. Most were wearing identical goggles, and some had green flippers glued to their shoes and green strips on pant legs and shirt sleeves. They marched into the *Ecole* behind a high stone wall and the wrought iron gates swung shut and that was the last I saw of them. I have no idea what it was all about. But there, in rural France on a Sunday afternoon, a frog parade. What are the odds?

Mont St. Michel

The outline of Mont St. Michel grows increasingly solemn and hypnotic as you approach. The spire-topped monolith offshore resembles a great and mysterious ship in the sea. Even as you get closer and begin to spot details – the abbey rooftops and the statue on the spire and the village at the base – it remains austere and ethereal. It seems not just from another time but from another world.

I skipped checking into the motel in favor of driving straight to the abbey. Mont St. Michel sits on its own island and it can be surrounded by the waters of the English Channel, but since the tide was out, I decided to hike around the entire structure. At the base it is all ancient rock and footpaths in the packed sand and mud. In troughs below the footpaths, fish stranded by the receding tide streak through the shallows. For all the centuries of habitation here, for 1200 years, the local people must have come to this spot to net the fish and collect the clams.

The circuit around Mont St. Michel, about two clicks, proved tiring, and I entered the main village, trudged past creperies and boutiques (the French word for boutique is, pronounced with a rising, lilting final syllable, "bout*ique*") A short flight of steps leads to the little church of St Pierre Eglise. The interior is cool and dim and lit with a thousand colored flickering candles. At the church door stands a metal, perhaps pewter, statue of Joan of Arc, fierce and heroic in armor and bobbed hair. But my feet hurt. Joan, *pardonnez moi*, we'll have to come back to you later.

After a nap and shower I felt better, and I made a pleasant dinner at the restaurant opposite my motel of moules (mussels) followed by a piscine stew – cod and shrimp with the head on plus julienne carrots and squash in a saffron sauce – accompanied by a modest dry Muscadet and topped off with Far Breton, a local specialty, a sort of plum cake with a custard bottom, served with cream.

It was still light outside and I tried to read on the patio but I was interrupted by singing from the brasserie across the street. The wait staff gathered near the fireplace, waitresses in trim gray dresses and waiters in spic-and-span black trousers with gray vests. They installed a microphone and then broke into a jolly, lilting French folksong. They began to get in the spirit. They hammed it up, struck poses and descended into terrible Maurice Chevalier impersonations. The singing degenerated into giggle-snorts, but the audience clapped enthusiastically and the vocalists struck up another tune. I imagined a similar sound from a group of beaver trappers in the North American woods, gathered around a camp fire, while someone squeezed a concertina, the grizzled, weary voyageurs belted out the same song. And then abruptly it ended. The waitresses tied on aprons and the waiters picked up trays. My heart leaped up and I wanted to shout "More, more, encore!" (The French word for encore is – heck – you know.) But the singers dispersed, and then a bagpipe began to wail a slow marching tune. I guessed that the bagpipe is not only a Scottish instrument, but also a part of local folk music. And then I retired to reflect on Breton, this small, kindly world.

This is Monday and today I became a *miquelot* and made pilgrimage to the great Abbey of Mont St. Michel. Now it is 1:30 p.m. amidst a spitting rain and I sit in the car to write up some notes of the visit and to wait for my weary feet to recompose themselves.

What can I say about Mont St. Michel that hasn't been said a hundred times before? You just have to see it for yourself, the awesome cathedral fortress emerging from the glistening sands of the surrounding sea. They call it the *Merveille L'Occident*, the Wonder of the West, and it leaves you in awe. Victor Hugo is quoted on a placard outside the quaint wax museum calling it *"un lieu quelle etrange"* and, though he was speaking of the irony that such a high holy place should become a political prison after the Revolution, he might have been speaking of Mont St. Michel at any time. This remote dot in the North Sea, an ancient burial ground known locally as Tomb Island, became by turns a lonely chapel to St. Michael and a Benedictine monastery and a Norman abbey and seat of power and a decrepit curio in the Restoration and a prison in the Revolution and finally a world landmark. Today it is a tourist haven visited by 850,000 people annually. There is a campground nearby, and a trailer park, and something called the "Mont St. Michel Reptilarium". It's a religious institution still, having a small Benedictine retreat reestablished here in 1965. It is layer upon layer of French history, a rude temple set up by St.

Aubert in 800 C.E. and built upon by Normans and Bretons and French in waves of aspiration.

I took the audio tour, and I suppose saw the usual sights, but what sticks with me are just flashes of things. I liked the small interior church to St. Peter and the tiny chapel to St. Aubert outside the walls on the seaside of the Abbey. I was intrigued by a huge wooden wheel in the old crypt area, used as a pulley to haul goods up 200 meters to the perch of the Benedictines – and a medieval conveyer belt, wooden roller bars hung in iron casings still draped outside the tower walls. The structure illuminates the daily feat of supplying food, water and everything to a religious retreat atop a 250-meter peak. I took photos of the graceful slate roofing on the shapely conical towers and the gold statue of St. Michael on the highest spire. The best room was the ingeniously lit Refectory with 57 (hidden) bay windows, and the best spot was the rose garden inside the cloisters. In the Knights Hall I looked up the fireplace to find an 80-foot tall chimney and giant stone flue.

There are museums within the museum, including a crummy wax museum that features prisoners in cells and kings in chambers and monks scribbling away in the Scriptorium. The best part of that side trip is a small garden outside the armor collection, hung with old newspaper clippings about the Abbey. One clipping from the 19th Century warns visitors to "eat the local salmon no more than three times per week."

I did a little souvenir shopping on the way out: a porcelain figurine and a Christmas tree ornament. (*Je voudrais une ornamente pour l'arbre de Bon Noel, s'il vois plais….* What?) There were gorgeous embroidered Breton shoes, sort of rainbow slip-ons, but I didn't know what size to buy. I bought a miniature plastic replica of Mont St. Michel, and then felt it was hokey and stuffed it in the bottom of my backpack. Leaning against the stone stairway, I watched the other tourists parading by: lots of Japanese, mostly groups all toting nifty cameras; sporadic Germans speaking loudly; Americans grumbling about the prices; a tour group of black children who spoke high-pitched French; and at the end of the pack a weary older woman who paused at the top of the steep stairway, sighed and said, "*Merde!*" Probably not French.

The off-and-on rain let up and I drove into Brittany and the village of St Malo. The first impression of the village was wonderful because I smelled jasmine. I could not locate the flower, and it was probably an illusion, but it made me think of a line from one of Guy de Maupassant's short stories. I forget the French of it, but he describes a young woman in the moonlight, walking through a garden "like a perfumed soul."

St. Malo

The guide book was not enthusiastic and I thought St Malo would be a bust, but it proved most pleasant. Avoiding the tiny wheeled tour-train that rolled through cobbled streets, I strolled along the old stone wall that encircled the port. Bracing salt air, pleasant view of rustic buildings and little churches and old hotels with blue shutters and a Napoleonic air. I had intended to walk to the ancient fort in the bay but the tide had risen and it was cut off by 50 meters of roiling sea. You could spot the access path rising up from the waves to the barred iron gate. Instead of wading I watched groups of school children receiving history lectures before antique carved wooden doors. Stylish locals dashed among the shops. At the *creperie* down at the water's edge, tacked on a wall was a child's poster of curly waves and bright-colored fish. The scrawled handwriting read *"La Mer est Blessee. Ne plus Polleur."* The sea is wounded. Don't pollute anymore.

From St Malo I drove to Dinan but stopped only for the motel. The main thing about Dinan is the wall. This medieval town of traders and artisans is perched 250 feet above the Rance River and encircled by a 30-40 foot wall. It has the most remaining ramparts of any village in France (held in place by wire mesh in a few spots). The wall is about 1.8 miles long (here I translate from the metric, because I wanted to size it up before I tried walking it, and as soon as it was converted to the measuring system of we backward Americans, I gave up the plan). The town interior includes half-frame Tudor-style houses which lean menacingly over the street.

At least I found a decent restaurant in town. Green salad with patty of minced salmon and chives; monkfish in lemon butter and small fillet of flounder; peeled potatoes and carrots; pear tart with whipped cream and almond slivers.

To my taste, however, Dinan was a bust, but that is where I had booked a room and that is where I slept. Uncomfortable Ibis motel chain room meant I had to lug my suitcase across the street from public parking and up two flights of stairs to a sad lumpy bed. I left Dinan next morning right after coffee because I had a long drive into the Loire Valley Tuesday. Something there is that doesn't love a wall.

The drive south perked me up, mostly because of the poppies. Flashing along roadsides, peeping from wheat field stubble, gushing from meadows, sprouting from sidewalk cracks, everywhere it was poppies, poppies, poppies. Their red-orange bloom is the color of overripe papaya. Here in France poppies are as common as dandelions back home – and come to think of it, I have seen no dandelions in France, so perhaps they have an understanding (the French word for "détente" is, okay, "détente"). From a conversation with a white-haired fellow years ago I learned that the veterans distribute artificial poppies on Armistice Day in memory of the millions killed in WWI. They say that you could tell where the bodies fell after a battle because there, over each shallow grave, the poppies would spring up. Maybe so. Or maybe the poppy is just a common weed over here, without need for an explanation. Still, it seems odd that poppies do not go wild in America. Maybe there is a governmental conspiracy to suppress poppies due to their interesting medicinal properties. Ian Fleming wrote a book entitled <u>The Poppy is Also a Flower</u>.

Poppies, poppies and roses, roses. And wild flowers. And gardens galore, flowers everywhere. The village of Dinan and several others announced themselves on entrance signs as "Ville Fleurie" – the way some American towns put up a sign at the entrance touting themselves as "Home of the 1997 State Girls Softball Champions". This seems like a harmless sort of boosterism, but I think I prefer the French version, bragging that one's hometown is flowerful.

Brittany

Saumur Chateau

Driving through Brittany (or is it Bretagne? Or is it Brittania?) seems less like Wisconsin. There are still 300-year-old stone outhouses, and herds of spotted cows, but the traffic moves faster and no farm equipment stalls the flow.

The strictly rural lifestyle seems to be falling away. I did see a road sign advertising "Le Tractor Pulling", but that seems phony as a rodeo in Dallas.

I stopped in Saumur to view my first chateau. It was beautiful, a blonde stone castle with blue-grey slate roof soaring above the Loire River valley. The interior was closed for repairs. The soft cream-colored limestone or "tufa" of Saumur may not wear so well as the gray granite of older medieval structures, or perhaps Saumur, like so many other chateaux, has simply been neglected. During lunch a flock of rooks soared in the chateau heights.

Nearby Chinon Chateau was a massive castle (and prison) now mostly rubble and ruins. It stands on Roman walls and in fact has been a fortress since Paleolithic times. If you want to get a feel for the place, you should check out the fine old costume drama "The Lion in Winter" which was set in 12th Century Chinon, when Henry II held his "Christmas Court" there. The film was not actually shot in the present-day ruin, but it has the atmosphere of pomp and dung characteristic of a medieval court.

Chinon has a storied past. Tradition says that Richard the Lion-Hearted died in Chinon after being wounded in 1199. A few centuries later it was the retreat of Charles VII, who was the Dauphin of a disputed throne during the 100 Years War. I stood in the very room where Joan of Arc visited the Dauphin and urged him to rally France and expel the invading English. Joan was later imprisoned across the courtyard in the Coudray Keep, and then transferred to Rouen for trial and burning. The French say the English killed her, and the English claim it was the French.

Just west of that Main Hall stands the prison tower or DonJon, which held among other notables one Jacques

DeMolay, the Grand Master of the Masonic order known as the Knights Templar. One can still see scratched high in the limestone of the dungeon DeMolay's name. Literature from the chateau museum states that DeMolay was imprisoned in the 14th Century by a king, Phillip the Fair, and that despite Pope Clement V's appeal, he was eventually tortured and killed. But my background says something different. My father was a Freemason, and in fact he hung around long enough and memorized enough ceremonious claptrap to become a minor functionary and a Shriner. When I was a pre-teen he encouraged me to join a Masonic youth group called the Demolays (DEE-moh-LAYS). We learned that poor Jacques was in fact imprisoned by the potentates of the Catholic Church, tortured to reveal the whereabouts of the Knights Templar treasury, and died at the stake, unrepentant and discrete. But what is the truth? who were the real murderers? was it the secular or the sacred authorities? Jacques DeMolay, Joan of Arc and I myself are all long past caring.

Chinon was effectively the capital of France while Burgundy (NE) and Normandy (semi-English) ruled the roost. After a century or so the capital moved to Paris and except for occasional state visits, Chinon was left to disintegrate.

Next I drove to Azay-le-Rideau to see the most beautiful of the chateau of my visit and a building of remarkable grace and elegance. Azay-le-Rideau is a prime example of the change in architecture that appeared with the French Renaissance, a dramatic contrast to the cold walls, creepy passages and gargoyle-studded towers of a place like Chinon. Azay-le-Rideau sits amid streams of the little Indra River and from a distance it seems to float on the water. I arrived too late to tour the interior, but I was content to stroll the extensive gardens and to marvel at the uncanny lightness of this massive (48 bedroom) home. The conical towers are topped with light ornate spires like candles on a birthday cake. The windows present a charming decoration in the façade and a promise of bright and livable quarters inside. The whole is reflected by the stream below like a tall-masted sailing ship in a pond.

I left the chateau late and with difficulty found my motel. Fatigue was beginning to catch up with me. Even the effort to speak French seemed like an imposition. At dinner I began the conversation with "Parlez-vous anglais?" and when the waitress didn't, I just pointed at items on the menu. The result was dismal: salad smothered with sliced pork and onions, some kind of poached fish with disgusting rice in chicken broth and, instead of the Bretagne specialty I ordered, a dish called La Flotante, I got fake Italian *tira misu*.

During a walk after dinner I approached the stone hill just behind the motel and found small houses carved into the hillside, each with a door and windows cut into living rock. Below the hill lay a gully that ran toward the hill, and at the hill base a small Roman arch leading to a black tunnel. From the mouth of the tunnel a bat emerged and flew into the moon.

Loire River Valley

Chimnies of Chateau d'Amboise

Today (Wednesday) is for plunging into the heart of chateau country, the valley of the Loire River. At daylight I veered a bit off course because I got lost around Tours and ended up mid-morning at Amboise, my destination for the evening. No problem. I parked my unstoppable Vauxhall Meriva near the chateau and slogged up yet another narrow cobblestone street and plunked down 5 Euros or so to enter the palatial Chateau d'Amboise. Like most of the 15th and 16th Century (Renaissance) buildings I saw, it was pale yellow stone with slate roof and cylindrical towers topped with a cone like a Wiley Coyote rocket. This place too was built over Roman and Medieval ruins and expanded to a massive castle with a commanding view of the Loire Valley. Standing on the ramparts I felt something like the twinge of power. I imagined how it would feel if all this were mine (or daddy's) – a gorgeous stone domicile bigger than a Howard Johnsons, with 60 chimneys and 300 servants and a dry moat to keep out insurance salesmen. Pretty heady stuff, this king of the castle and lord of the realm stuff, and I swelled with a sense of my own importance. Or maybe that was the fried onions. It gave me a sense of majesty to gaze at my vast holdings and to realize that I could spit on any of the 200 tourists swarming below.

My first stop on the chateau tour was a small chapel decked out with crenellated towers and protruding gargoyles and modest spires. I began to get a feel for what the guide book called the "Renaissance style" of architecture because this place was a mixture of the late medieval (gargoyles) and the lighter, more graceful new style (conical towers with caps like upturned lilies). The chapel was lighted by stained glass windows (replaced since German air raids of WWII), and overhead the entwined gothic arches were thinner, lighter, airier than the ones at Chinon. I followed a steep, winding ramp up to the courtyard, a passage suitable for knights in full armor riding three abreast, and at last found myself on the inside of a chateau. The first room or Knight's Room held the guards who kept out rabble (like me). Smaller rooms leading off the wide entrance held sticks of ornate carved wooden furniture, drab tapestries, a couple of fancy floor-to-ceiling 4-poster beds draped with heavy cloth. On the walls hung halberds and portraits of ancient big-wigs – and I kid you not, one of those wigs would have filled three French bathrooms.

One chair caught my eye because it differed markedly from the thick, rectilinear medieval furniture, the heavy and square stuff dating from the 13th Century. This chair was of light wood with a curved and padded seat, and the back was carved with a landscape in perspective. It blended the two eras into one: the lions-claw chair legs were gothic, but the scene in *trompe-d'oeil* perspective was strictly a Renaissance contribution.

Little of the furniture was original to the chateau, since the royalty of the Renaissance was itinerant. They moved with the seasons – or the political winds – from castle to castle.

The mix of architectural and decorative art styles raises a recurring question, not unlike the one posed by the Golden Age of ancient Greece: just what caused the change from Medieval style to the burst of creativity and lightness in the Renaissance? What happened and who did it and why?

This was the topic of a fascinating, frustrating book that a friend recommended that I read during my tour of Renaissance France, The Waning of the Middle Ages by J. Huizinga. It was fascinating because it described in elaborate detail the character of Medieval France and Holland, but it was frustrating because I wanted to argue several points, and since it was published in 1924, it was probably too late to send an email query to the author. The book exhibits extraordinary erudition – Huizinga seems to have read everything written in Middle French, including sermons, innkeeper account books and the menus for church feasts. It is excellent history because it evokes with imagination the textures of an historical period, like the description of multitudinous church bells ringing across the valley of the Loire. But it also contains some dubious aesthetic theories, and an explanation of Chivalry and Romantic Love that simply does not jibe with my experience.

The thesis of The Waning of the Middle Ages is that the Renaissance has roots in, was clearly anticipated by, what most historians would call the late Medieval Period in France (roughly 14th and 15th Century). Okay, well and good. Huizinga points to all the things we associate with that culture, the overwhelming influence of Christian thought in politics and society, the dominant taste for symbolism (heraldry, icons, proverbs, allegory), the feudal and agrarian economy; and he shows that the latter stages of those trends promoted the rediscovery of classical science and empiricism and human proportions -- the intellectual blossoming we call the Renaissance.

All this seems teleological or circular reasoning. First, you abstract from the continuum of history a couple of chunks of time – call them Medieval and Renaissance – and you define them as distinct and coherent -- and then you argue that they are, omygosh, causally related. It's as though Huizinga created his own allegory, the story of Dame Late Middle Ages and Dame Renaissance, and then discovered that they were Siamese twins!

Still, labels are useful, and something was happening between the time of Notre Dame Cathedral and the time of Chateau d'Amboise. At Notre Dame the gargoyles were powerful magic -- icons to ward off demons. In the Renaissance, gargoyles were a quaint glance back at a time of relative simplicity and certainty. My guess is that understanding the character of both Medieval and Renaissance thought might come from understanding the psychological makeup of a person who bridged both eras, a person like Leonardo da Vinci, who was steeped in Middle Ages piety and yet broke out of that mindset to become the quintessential "renaissance man". [More about Leonardo later, after I visit Clos Luce.]

Chenonceau Chateau

After Chateau d'Amboise I drove to yet another chateau. The one at Chenonceau was bigger, certainly, with add-on wings connected by great hallways and the whole shebang set inside a moat made from the Char River. It had the same accessories – the tapestries and 4-poster beds and ornate clothes chests – but it also had a woman's touch in the graceful chandeliers and decorative floors. Much of the chateau was designed by Catherine Medici, the mother of five queens and a notorious power monger of the Renaissance. Chenonceau had extensive gardens including one section planted entirely in pink rose trees. The pink roses and the finery gave the place a distinctively feminine air. My favorite part was the Great Hall connecting sections of the chateau. During WWI the Great Hall was donated to the nation for use as an infirmary. Recuperating patients used to fish out the windows in the Char River below. During WWII the Great Hall played a very interesting role because the north end lay in the Nazi Occupied Zone and the south end lay in Vichy.

From the ramparts of Chenonceau I could look out over the valley and spot three or four vineyards. On the way out I stopped at the local *cave* or wine cellar. The museum sold bottles of wine made from grapes grown on the grounds. I tasted some new Chardonay, some pretty new Gamay and a nice old Cabernet. I looked for some place to spit out the sample wine, because that's the way it's done in movies, but finding nowhere to unload it, I just gulped it down. I bought three bottles of the Gamay with grassy overtones – a real bargain at 8 Euros.

Incidentally, the French call their wine cellars *caves* because they often store wine in literal caves, great hollows in the limestone embankments of the Loire River. Since pre-history the French have inhabited such caves, and in more modern times they have found the caves a cool dry place to keep wine. The French word for "cave" is obviously "cave", but it means more than "cave".

Chateau de Clos Luce

After Chenonceau I drove back to Amboise and went straight to the Chateau de Clos Luce (or, as it used to be called, the manor at Cloux). It includes the cultural park dedicated to Leonardo da Vinci. Leonardo, as we familiars call him, was part of the brain drain that brought Italian Renaissance thinkers to France. He had made a name for himself as a painter and engineer in Florence and Sforza, and toward the end of his life (1516) King Francis I of France lured him from Italy to a chateau in the Loire Valley to help jump start the French Renaissance. He lived three years in the chateau, painting and designing fortifications and scribbling furiously in his renowned notebooks. He was buried in the big house, the Chateau d'Amboise up on the hill, and in fact I walked by his grave (probably) when I toured the chapel of the chateau.

The tour of his residence delights literary types, since the walls are hung with pithy quotations from his notebooks. The bedroom, the kitchen and the spacious study preserve his furniture and personal effects. The small but exquisite rose garden in his courtyard is a fine place to sip *café au lait*. The patrons of visual arts can enjoy an open-air discussion of his painterly evolution at an auditorium in the woods, complete with flapping panels hung in the trees of Grimacing St. Jerome, Darning Mary and Smiling Mona Lisa. The basement floor delights the engineer types, since the floor is packed with models of his ingenious machines, donated by IBM. The working models of a bicycle and swinging drawbridge and ball bearings astound us to this day. In the park behind the chateau stand life-sized machines based on his design, and the visitor is invited to operate them and marvel at his prescience. There is a screw-shaped helicopter blade and a five-meter high millwheel used as a pulley and paddleboats on the pond and a pyramid-shaped parachute hanging from the chestnut trees. I liked especially his design for a bilge pump, consisting of a huge lever attached to a spoon-shaped strip of waterproof canvas which, plunged like a dip net into the pond, filled with water and then was easily lifted with levers and drained away.

Departing the home of Leonardo, one cannot help but marvel at the breadth of his achievements. We have all read a book or an article – or seen that silly movie – about his idiosyncratic personality. He wrote and painted with either hand. He designed a bat-winged aircraft that, if manufactured, would weigh 500 pounds – and it was to be powered by human muscles. He deduced from dissections, mostly animal, that sperm was created in the bone marrow. He called war a *pazzia bestialissima*, a most bestial folly, and yet he invented a fan gun, a bombard, an improved catapult and a series of clever and lethal fortification defenses. He had, to put it mildly, an original mind.

At the same time, he was intensely, almost conventionally, pious. He thought God the source of light and that the

78

painter in capturing the qualities of light was exalting God. He accepted Aristotle's concept of four elements and yet he insisted on empirical methods and all art based "on science". He had a Medieval disdain for sex and yet (see Leda) he produced the erotic sublime. Leonardo was a Pythagorean vegetarian, but he waxed indignant about cruelty to plants. In short, he was a mixed bag.

So what is it about him, as representative of the Renaissance, that makes him so different from his predecessors of the Middle Ages? He did not come from nowhere, even his inventions. Marco Cianchi in his book <u>Leonardo da Vinci's Machines</u> writes that "Leonardo's technological drawings often draw on other writer's books and manuscripts.... while his mechanics and engineering are, for their breadth and depth of experience, unique and at times ahead of their times, they are not fruit ripened all alone in a desert." He combined voracious reading and the best ideas of antiquity with his own inventiveness and daring, to create things never before seen. Maybe that is the key to the man and the era: intellectual courage.

In his notebooks Leonardo continually urges painters to observe keenly, to look hard, to see what is actually there and not to see preconceptions of what is there. Our preconception of a roof line is that it must be rectilinear, but close observation shows that it is rhomboidal, that its lines recede to a point in the distance. This yields perspective, or in the words of T.S. Eliot, the only possible meaningful achievement in life, a better "approximation of reality."

It comes from daring to really look.

Thursday, I awoke with the roosters and took a backyard walk that discovered warblers, magpies and lots of pigeons. The French word for pigeon is – well, c'mon. Honeyed morning sunlight streamed over the neighbor's wheat. At the back of the Da Vinci Museum sits a small building like a silo only built with wooden ribs connected by flat bricks, forming hundreds of niches just the right size for a bird's nest. It is called Le Pigeonieree.

Okay, I have put it off as long as I can. Time for the History of France in twenty-five words or so. France is a big chunk of Old Europe "slightly less than twice the size of Colorado" (CIA World Fact Book), and unique in having coasts on both the North Sea and the Mediterranean. It is laced with tame rivers like the Seine and Loire gently flowing through verdant valleys and rocky hills. The land is rich, and in fact France contains some of the longest continuously inhabited regions of the world, including the troglodyte dwellings around Lascaux, famous for 20,000-year-old cave paintings of a big-assed horse. Tribal peoples like the Franks and Gauls traipsed around the place for thousands of years looking for truffles until, about the year zero, Julius Caesar and the boys invaded and set up camp. You will remember from Caesar's commentaries that *"Omnia Gallia in partis tres divisa est"* – and Rome filled those three parts of Gaul with roads, viaducts, bridges, temples, fortifications, Christianity, etc.

Things fell apart for Rome, and the Gauls spent centuries warring among themselves until about 700 A.D. when Charlemagne (or, as we say in the USA, "Big Charlie") united the warring tribes, established central rule and had himself crowned King of the Holy Roman Empire. The people had taken to speaking Latin, in imitation of their conquerors, only a poofy version of it called French.

More wars, mayhem, boar hunting and wine making ensued, and pretty soon the French found themselves in the Middle Ages – only they didn't call it the Middle Ages because they were in the middle of it. They called it Hard Times. You had to be deaf and a hunchback to find a job. They held a Hundred Years War with England that lasted 114 years (because it was the Dark Ages and people couldn't count). Things were grim, what with hunger, incessant wars, the plague, witch hunts and a lack of decent toilet paper, and so the French built castles for defense and Gothic cathedrals to get right with God and, to pass the time, they invented chivalry, monasticism, etiquette and Romantic Love.

Still, the French were not content, so they staged a Renaissance (16th Century) wherein they knocked down castles to put up chateaux, drank more wine, danced the minuet and created their most important contribution to culture: French cuisine. The Renaissance rolled into the Enlightenment wherein people amassed empirical knowledge in Encyclopedias and wore big funny wigs. They colonized parts of the New World and got heap big piles of beaver pelts, but the project fizzled. And everyone was having a good time except for the French people, who were getting pretty tired of hauling water up to the chateaux on the hill, and so they ousted the aristocracy, chopped off the king's head and called it the French Revolution (1789). Things went from bad to worse until a short Corsican named Napoleon wrangled himself an army and set off to conquer the world. However, the world objected and penalized the French with the 19th Century, during which period the government wobbled between restoring and deposing monarchy, the business types set up colonies in Africa, Asia and the Caribbean, and engineers built the Suez Canal and the Eiffel Tower.

Comes the 20th Century, and the French are happily snubbing tourists when suddenly their neighbors, those mischievous Germans, clobber them with not one but two world wars. Champagne becomes cheaper than gasoline.

The French are so depressed that they get themselves booted out of Algeria and Viet Nam and become a spoilsport in the U.N, and that is pretty much where it remains today.

That's my History of France, and if you don't like it – go buy a book.

Thursday was supposed to be dedicated to three or four more chateaux, but I was feeling chateau'd up the whazoo, so I tottled down to the riverbank and rented a canoe. The current of the Loire was mild enough that a person could paddle against it and make headway, but I was happy just letting the craft float down the river. The banks held a few fishermen, a few lovers, but mostly wildflowers. I sang to myself, "Ahh – louetta, gentile alouette."

Mid-morning I hit the road for Chambord. Generally, I have enjoyed my hours driving through France, despite the narrow and steep (*rappel*) roads, frequent interruptions by traffic circles and maddening road signs. For the last 20 years the only time I have driven a stick shift is in Europe, and I find exercising that small, quiet skill faintly nostalgic and satisfying. The countryside floats by like a reverie: tiny stone bridges over gentle streams, quaint churches, little ivy-covered inns, fields of straw-colored wheat and silver rye and reddish barley. Except around the American cemetery at the Normandy beaches, I don't recall seeing any field planted in corn – maize. My skies were mostly blue with cotton candy clouds. Everywhere the flowers nodded by the roadside – Queen Anne's lace and blue cornflowers and yellow sunflowers. Poppies galore. There was an especially pleasant village at Coeur Civerny with a modest chateau, vibrant green golf course and small kempt vineyards. On one of those notoriously narrow country lanes – about two cows wide – I spotted coming from the opposite direction a large speeding truck. There is no place to pull over (*rives dangerous*) and no time to stop and it is bearing down on me at hellish speed and so I gritted my teeth like a knight on a charger approaching a joust. The truck roared by and its breeze made my car tremble. I suppose that a miss of a millimeter is good as a mile, but it leaves a shudder in its wake.

The Chateau de Chambord is the one Henry James called "the most royal of chateaux". Unlike the others I visited, it sits on no river and it is surrounded by no moat. Instead the Chateau is surrounded by a vast forested park, almost the size of all Paris. It has huge lawns, stable grounds large enough for horse shows, and wooded sections that used to serve as the royal hunting grounds. A sign on the drive from the highway suggests that big game, stag and boar, still roam at will in the woods (*Attention: faunes sauvages a liberte*).

The chateau has 438 rooms and 78 fireplaces and a motley collection of tapestries, uncomfortable furniture and royal portraiture in every one. That Louis XIV was truly a homely man. If he weren't king of France, he couldn't get a date.

I skipped most of Chambord's 438 rooms, thank you, having had a bellyful of chateaux, but I paused in the bed chamber of the last royal occupant. Le Compte de Chambord was all set in the 19th Century to become King. The people were unhappy with the government, the economy was strained, and many urged the restoration of monarchy and crowning of Henry V of France. But at the last minute, after years of negotiation and preparation, the Count refused to accept the flag of the French Revolution, the tricolor, as his ensignia. He felt it was a dishonor to the royal house, and so he returned to exile never again to enter France. He remained all his life only a Pretender to the throne.

Chartres

Driving northeast to Chartres, now definitely closing the loop to Paris, I got bamboozled in Blois and had to stop at a tollway cafe to check my map. To my surprise I got fast food at the rest stop, a small cherry tart (*tartelette cerise*) and coffee in five minutes. At the outdoor table I fed the exceedingly tame sparrows who seemed to be chirping in French.

Chartres is a city with a whopping big church. The Cathedral started in the 4th Century as a Gallo-Roman wall, got expanded in the 6th, 8th and 11th Centuries, burned in the 12th and took its massive final form in the 13th. The flamboyant gothic steeple 115 meters tall was added in the 16th Century. (French word for flamboyant is the same as English, only pronounced wrong). All those centuries, and they forgot to put in bathrooms.

Since I arrived in Chartres late afternoon, the gigantic stained-glass windows lacked a flood of sunlight, and the cathedral interior was gloomy. In fact the whole town of Chartres seemed to me shabby and worn. Perhaps the impression came from my seedy motel about 100 meters from the cathedral and near the bus station. I strolled past a fine memorial of a gigantic raised fist clutching a broken sword and dedicated to a leader of the Chartres *resistance*. Then I took in a movie, a schmaltzy cartoon called "Cars," enlivened by the French dialogue and the sexy commercials shown during the previews.

When I emerged from the theatre it was dark, as I had planned, since I wanted to see the light show at the cathedral (*Chartres en Lumieres*). But I had forgotten to eat since *petit dejuner*, and I was famished, and all the interesting restaurants were closed. I bought a kebab at a walk by stand (spiced lamb and fries, like a gyro without the piquant cucumber sauce) and munched from a park bench while I watched the *Lumieres*. Probably scandalized the locals. The light show consisted of running spotlights up and down the cathedral and then imposing a colorful slide of Jesus and angels on the façade of the church while all the time blasting from loudspeakers sacred music by Handel. It struck me as neither beautiful nor spiritual, but it attracted a crowd of fifty or so curious onlookers. It reminded me of Samuel Johnson's observation after hearing a woman preach. "It was like watching a dog walk on its hind legs, not that it was done well, but astonishing that it was done at all."

Paris

The drive from Chartres to Paris went quickly, a little over two hours, and I guessed right about navigating around Paris and got to my hotel at Charles De Gaulle Airport by 10 a.m. My room was not ready and so I charged my camera battery in the hotel lobby while I took in the expansive buffet lunch. Two French businessmen at the table next to me talked mile a minute and downed a liter of wine. They both wore lightweight suits with blue shirts and yellow polka-dot ties. Parisians look chic and on the make.

I took the hotel shuttle to the Metro station and then a 45-minute train ride to the Notre Dame station. Emerged from the tube to join Friday morning swarm of tourists around the lovely old Cathedral. Walking along the Seine I saw a Japanese fellow with a fiberglass pole hook a fish and then pull in a 15-inch long squirming eel. Children on the riverbank squealed with delight.

Next I hoofed it past the Louvre and arrived at my target destination for the afternoon, the Musee D'Orsay, an old train station that has been converted to an art museum. The design of the museum is ideal, since the old train station has a high vaulted glass ceiling that allows natural light to stream down on scores of Neoclassical statues in the center. The collection, to my taste, was at first disappointingly predictable, and the adjoining rooms at the sides held ho-hum work, an unfinished Degas and a few lesser Courbets. I took the escalator up to the fifth floor and there, unfolding before me like the path to paradise, hung a magnificent collection of Impressionist paintings.

They had hundreds, it seemed like miles, of beautiful Manet, Renoir, Pissarro, Monet and Degas works. Two rooms of Monet alone, including a large almost Expressionist abstract of the Giverny lily pond and an earlier painting of a city street vibrant with waving tricolor flags. I discovered a new hero, Henri Fantin-Latour, a talented Impressionist portrait painter whose work I had never seen before. I wallowed in it, gorged on it, grooved and gassed about it, until the P.A. system announced that the museum would begin closing in fifteen minutes. Then I raced toward the back of the hall and discovered a dozen unexplored rooms thick with masterpieces. A hall of Seurat and the Pointillists, but no time to look, an intriguing gallery of Odion Radon and other Post-impressionists, but I was zooming, a room of Gauguin where I feasted like a starving man and then ran on to confront a half dozen sublime Cezanne still-lifes. The art guardians shooed me out, but I promised myself to return.

I had a beer or two at a convenient café while my heart quit pounding and my aching feet quit throbbing. The couple sitting at the table next to me were Americans. They did not even try to speak French, just "Gimme a coffee and for the lady a glass uh white wine." They dressed in shorts and t-shirts, they were hot and sweaty and grossly overweight. [Note to self: lose 20 pounds immediately – no excuses – if only for the sake of international relations.] After the couple left, I spoke only French, called for my bill and complimented the place on the onion soup. The waiter smiled indulgently, aware that I was trying to compensate for the Ugly Americans. I think he added four Euros to my bill.

The train ride back to my hotel was odd because it contained mostly dark-skinned passengers. The passenger cars were crowded until one or two stops from the airport, when all the blacks got off, the women in bright print dresses and heavy jewelry and head bands, the men in baggy dungarees and work boots. I developed a theory about that demographic. It appeared that this group was French-African, based on the dress and the cell phone conversations, and the fact that, sitting in small groups, they spoke some alien tongue (Bantu, or maybe Swahili?) but they shouted across the aisle in French.

I figured that they were the French equivalent of the itinerant Mexicans in the USA; they were a source of cheap labor. At the end of a long workday they ride to the furthest (cheapest) suburbs served by the Metro trains. They dress in practical clothing, and they shuck off the labors of the day with the cheapest of diversions, conversation. They are the invisible folks who clean your toilettes, O Ma Belle France, and sweep up your cigarette butts, and haul your trash. They are the peasants of the new global economy, the landless, the penniless, the wretched refuse of far teeming shores yearning to breathe free. And I reflected that I myself, and the pale-skinned Parisians around me, are the new elite. We travel farther and faster than the kings of yore. We eat better. We have at our fingertips more books, more medicine, and more gorgeous art than Louis Quatorze in all his glory. These folks may not be starving and flea-ridden like the

Medieval peasants (and the folks back home), but the world is still a cruel merry-go-round of Haves and Have-Nots.

And yet there is wealth enough to go around if only we share. That's why I am a liberal and a believer in the slow arduous climb up from bestiality to humanity. Will Rogers wrote that "The Democrats, like the poor, will be with us always."

Sitting in the airport waiting room, after perilously navigating the spiral-shaped ramps of the CDG rental car return (interesting but impractical – the French, after all, brought us the Concorde SST, and the Eiffel Tower says all you need to know about French engineering), I try to make sense of my Normandy travels. What is the theme? It might be flowers, since they abounded, and the French royal emblem was a fleur-de-lis, and the most influential book of the Middle Ages was a French meditation on chivalry and idyllic love called the Romance of the Rose.

Maybe the theme is not flowers but rather the invention of love. While the Bayeaux tapestry was being stitched the French were devising something more lasting. Foremost among the nations of Europe the French defined, distilled and perfected the ideal of courtly love. Our notions of Arthurian chivalry are mainly French hand-me-downs. The obsession with perfect virtue in the Church – ideals of selflessness, chastity and devotion – were translated into secular ideals of courtship. In France the quest for the Holy Grail was confounded with the quest for the Maiden Fair, and the age-old attraction between the sexes reached heroic dimensions. It has echoed down the centuries, so that France today is still a land of roses, bedroom farce and *toujours l'amour*. (The English for *toujours l'amour* does not exist.)

Another theme might be the emergence of the Renaissance. The flying buttresses of Chartres and Notre Dame (and let's face it, the image of Lon Chaney swinging on the bell in "Hunchback of You-Know-Who") made me rethink the cause behind that "clean break", that cultural transformation we call the Renaissance. The dark, creepy corridors of the DonJon at Chinon, the instruments or torture displayed at Mont St. Michel, the centuries of feudal oppression, the mind-numbing handicrafts representing endless toil by masons, glass workers, scribes and weavers – even the execution of a country maid who dared to play soldier – all that tortured piety and superstition – suddenly cast off in favor of empirical knowledge and joy in learning, the age of Galileo and Columbus and of course, Leonardo. Did it come from a kind of courage? And if intellectual courage is rare in a man, how much rarer to find it at large in society?

Or maybe the theme is liberty. The French Revolution occurred after the American, but many Frenchmen argue that ours didn't really count. The American Revolution was largely a tax revolt, and in a colony on a different continent, and so the estrangement was understandable and practical. If King George III had quit soaking the colonists with stamp taxes and tea taxes, we might today be singing "God Save the Queen".

But in France the revolt went to the bone. All the centuries of aristocratic abuse, all the lies and organized exploitation, all the abject collusion of the state-run Church went up in flames, along with the notion of a sacred, anointed monarch and a permanently privileged class. And it took a bloody horrible purgative to cast off that entrenched social organization. The French Revolution was a revolt of the human spirit, a class war, and a declaration of universal human rights that shook Europe to the core. The American Revolution was viewed as a parochial spat, an aberrance, but the French version changed our ideas of the social contract forever.

All those chateaux I visited, so elegantly designed and furnished, represent a change in taste and outlook for those who have leisure for taste and outlook. But the privileged perches were built on the labors of suffering masses. The Renaissance brought a change in intellect for many, but the Revolution brought a change in the soul of the nation. Chivalrous ideals of fair play, honor, justice and grace were finally extended to all. *Liberte, egalite, fraternite.* What a concept.

And then, of course, came the reality check known as World War I.

So, what is the theme of my trip to northern France? Is it roses and chivalry? Is it Medieval industry or Renaissance intellect? Is it just plain wine and good food and bikinis?

France is a good place for people. Rich harvests from coast to coast, bountiful fields between, apples and pears and grapes for the picking. And if people don't mess it up with pollution or intolerant religion or greedy government, then it will remain for a long time a place to enjoy some frothy coffee and conversation, munch a crunchy salad and an apple tart, gaze at proud buildings and gorgeous art. It is a place to loosen your shoes, sip a noble wine, inhale the salt air and maybe -- who knows – to fall in love with life.

Side Trips

Basel

After an 8-hour flight plus an hour layover in Zurich plus another hour delay before the baby jet zipped 20 minutes back west to Basel, I made it to my hotel room on the Clarastrasse at 11:30 a.m. – 4:30 a.m. biological time. I flopped into bed and slept like a grumpy baby for three hours. I was determined to get first impressions of Switzerland while there was still daylight, so I jumped in the shower, dressed in jeans and a sport coat, and hit the street.

Actually, first impressions of the alien country began long before I walked the streets. The Zurich airport had free newspapers (in Frankfort they have free coffee), and the airport terminals were bristling with chocolate shops. When I emerged from my taxi, I saw my first Swiss child – I don't know what I was expecting, maybe a boy in *liederhosen* or a girl with a milkmaid's embroidered vest – but this was a black kid about nine whizzing past me on a collapsible titanium scooter. Welcome to Switzerland and watch your toes.

The hotel room also provided a vaguely alien experience. No chain lock on the door but a deadbolt that looked serious. The room key was not a plastic reprogrammable card, like in America, but a stainless steel real key, attached to an 8-inch long slab of plastic. Losing that room key would be like losing an arm. You would notice. The room had a TV made by the cell phone company, Nokia, and it had the predictable sitcoms and news shows in German, French and Italian. The in-room bar had Perrier, Heineken and the inevitable Toblerone chocolates. The bath was tiny but efficient, with crummy soap, rough toilet paper, and a sign in German suggesting that I save the world, or at least the rain forests, by recycling my used towels.

On the street the signs were mostly German too. Taverns serving *bier* and clothing stores and drugstores (*apoteke*) and jewelry (*bijou und goldschmiel*) music and shoes (*schuse*) and haircuts and of course candy stores (*confiserie*). Some of the hipper joints had English signs to signify their hipness. A bistro called Jazzabo proclaimed an ambience "just like a New York loft" (god forbid) and about halfway down the block was a club called "Sexy Crazy Center" which sold either girls or shoes. At the intersection of Feldbergstrasse at a tram stop sat an old couple; the man had a cane and a gray fedora and the woman had black hose and a purple print dress. Next to them young men in black leather coats sat quietly conversing in alternate German and French. The electric trolley arrived and they all boarded and when the trolley lurched away the corner was deserted except for me and three sparrows.

Further west on the Clarastrasse I crossed the Rhine (*Rhein*) River. According to the guide books, Basel is a town that happened 800 years ago because there was a wide place in the river. It happens all the time, you come to a bend in the river and the water slows down, and all sorts of debris including human habitation are deposited there. At Basel the Rhine is not so wide as the Mississippi at Alton, but wider than the Des Plaines at Des Plaines. A pleasant river scene that reminded me of the Seine, with molded concrete edging all along the bank and lovers there basking in the slightly chill April sunshine and smoking and kissing. From the middle of the Clarastrasse bridge I could see two more bridges, each with graceful parabolic arches and small flags flying. Small motor boats were plying the river in both directions and in the middle a large flat-bottomed barge plowed north with some massive cargo. On the far side of the bridge I found a kiosk rudely stapled over with flyers that advertised summertime cruises on the Rhine with lovely views, food and beer and "mit der Musik Dixieland".

The west side of the Rhine was the old town. Many of the streets dead-ended in a cobbled clear space, like a town square, with a simple fountain with running spigots and a tub about the size adequate to water horses. The old 13th Century town hall (*rathaus*) stood out with brightly colored tiles on the roof and crenellated -- or is it tessellated? -- anyway, spikey protrusions along the ridges of the spires. The stone walls held elaborately painted murals that depicted medieval scenes of soldiers and maidens and priests. An especially good likeness of two Great Danes lolling before a fireplace. My poor German was overwhelmed by the task of interpreting the various historical markers and the slogans painted on the walls. The one motto which I think I understood was about freedom: "Freiheit ist uber silber und gold."

On a large pedestal at the entrance of the *rathaus*, and again depicted in a couple of the murals, was the figure of a gray-bearded, grizzled man in armor. He had fierce eyes, an expression like someone had just committed a nuisance next to him in an enclosed elevator, and he wore a hat festooned with drooping egret feathers. Altogether, he was a ludicrous figure, a cross between Don Quixote and an angry chicken, and I was smirking in his direction when I caught myself. They say that travel is broadening, and as I gazed at that comical historical figure, I reflected on what an alien might make of a statue of an American hero, Davy Crockett, in his coonskin cap. And suddenly, right there in the middle of a Basel town square, I felt a great affection for the Swiss, and for all people who erect statues to their forefathers. We are brothers in the blood and sisters under the skin, profoundly alike, spiritually kindred and inextricably linked by the bonds of our own and mutual ridiculousness.

Walking on brought me to a sort of entertainment district. There were movie theatres showing "What Women Want", "Proof of Life" and "Thirteen Days". The hands-down favorite movie in Basel – you guessed it – "Chocolat". I thought it might be fun to see 13 Days with Kennedy played by Kevin Costner spouting German, but it wasn't showing again for over an hour and it cost 16 francs ($9.60) and so I passed. I ducked into a games arcade where there were a few pinball machines and pinball-sized electric kung fu games, but where most of the patrons were sitting in front of ordinary PCs, wearing headphones and playing PC-based car racing or NBA basketball simulation or gladiator whomping or electronic kung fu. Maybe the attraction was gaming on the Internet, and maybe some of those kids were hooked into Tangiers or Chicago. But it struck me as ironic: here were the teenagers smack in a pleasant, interesting prime reality, and they preferred a shabby form of virtual reality. Shrug, sigh, I walked on.

It began to rain. The sad Confederate gray sky just gave up the ghost and let it all hang out and down it came in patter and then plops. I found myself hunched beneath an awning as I watched people scurry in the shower. Behind me stood an espresso shop, and so I sat in a sturdy steel-and-pine folding chair and ordered a coffee (Ich mochte bitte ein Tasse Kaffee mit Milch) and then I caught myself and ordered a chocolate. The rain came tumbling down, and I watched the Swiss get wet, some folks with black bumbershoots but most just bare-headed teenagers walking and talking with great animation as though unconsciously exulting to be caught in the rain. A solemn doe-eyed waitress brought my hot chocolate, and I beamed at the saucer she left. It was perfect. A great white porcelain mug filled with steaming liquid; a cap of foamed milk and atop that a film of grated chocolate. I spooned up some foam and it was all heady fragrance, earthy as chocolate and heavenly as cream. Then I drank. The chill rainy air made the warmth welcome and intensified the tastes, and I cooed with creature comfort. It was delicious, a perfect balance of bitter and sweet, the very taste of life itself.

Sunday I slept late, trying to convince myself that it was 6 a.m. when my body thought it was 3 a.m. and the sun thought it was 10 a.m. We were all hopelessly confused but we managed to stumble into the shower and make it to breakfast before the hotel dining parlor closed. Those peculiar European scrambled eggs, runny as curdled milk. Liver sausage for breakfast, for crying out loud. Six kinds of cheese. I made breakfast of lunchmeat, a cheese like brie, croissant and coffee. Not bad actually; it would be good to stock some brie in the home refrigerator.

This day I walked west again, across the Rhine and past the old Rathaus into the cultural district. I was headed straight for the Art Museum (Kunstmuseum) but my path took me through narrow cobbled lanes, past a thousand pleasant boutiques, perfumeries and swatch shops and multiple chocolate shops, and of course I dawdled. Almost all the shop windows had Easter decorations. Plenty of cut flowers and cellophane-wrapped chocolates; also *papier mache* bunnies, painted wooden tulips and ceramic chicks and stuffed silk lambs. Eager to join the celebration, I bought a silk tie dotted with pastel tulips. So far, Easter in Basel presented itself as cheerful, chocolate-covered Christianity.

The Kunstmuseum was exactly as the guidebook had promised: small but excellent. The whole museum was about the size of the Impressionist collection at the Art Institute of Chicago, but in that limited space they managed to pack several wonderful impressionists, and also some fine expressionists and some medieval and some modern. It wasn't pretentious and it wasn't quaint; it was what it ought to be, a quiet out-of-the-way treasure house of beautiful objects.

 The ground floor had a special exhibit of Alberto Giacometti, three rooms filled with his characteristic skinny sculptures, also some bizarre carnival masks and a few monochrome oil paintings. Formerly I thought of Giacometti as Italian, but in this setting, with so much Giacometti in one place, he became Swiss-Italian. But then, art has no nationality.

A clamber up an appalling flight of stairs to the second floor, brought a modest reward of oil paintings, mostly Medieval and a bit of early Renaissance. The largest contributor was some guy named Wirz who was from Basel and who liked to paint Mary suckling baby Jesus and haloes all around. Not my cup of tea. Then there were scores of canvases by anonymous medieval painters – der Meister von Gluttenberg, der Meister von Lieptizig, der Meister von Basler. Dull, duller and dullissimo. Except for one dual painting, triptych I think it's called, which is two side-by-side portraits which comment on each other. In this case one portrait showed a plump blonde fellow in medieval tunic, rather a goof, and next to it was the same figure, only shown as a decomposing body. It was the same size as the portrait, and it had the same tilt to the chin, only it was a skull instead of a face, and a mummified body with exposed rib bones instead of robes. It was sort of gruesome; the mummified body had burst apart in places and gnarly worms were poking out. Five hundred year old art can still put us plump, contented goofs in our places. Medieval artists saw beneath our robes to the mortal bones, our inherent and possibly poignant ridiculousness.

The third floor, up another imposing flight of stairs, was all 20th Century and some delightful stuff. Dozens of Georges

Braque, followed by dozens of Picasso. Mostly mediocre Picasso, but one still life (*nature morte*) of bread on a table that was a work of undeniable genius. A couple of oils by a painter I don't know, Franz Marc, but whose stuff reminds me of Kandinsky and is a joy. A score of small canvases by Paul Klee; one Modigliani and a couple of Bonnards; several Chagall including one that is a breathtaking portrait of a young woman called "My Fiancee in Black Gloves". The paintings exemplified the variety and interconnections of 20th Century art. The Basel exhibit showed that modern schools of art were a lively stew of styles. There is Chagall painting in the Cubist style of Picasso, and there is Picasso imitating Miro; there's Klee as Roth and there goes Picasso again, out-expressing the Expressionists. It must have been fun, and competitive, and artistically exhilarating to have lived in Paris in the 20's and to jostle with so many mutually incompatible and yet mutually valid visions.

And what a treat to find in Basel. The guidebook tells me that Basel is the second largest city in Switzerland (after Zurich) with a population of 200,000. Okay, that makes it the size of Rockford, Illinois. But see the difference in expectations and quality of life! Imagine Rockford with even one Picasso, much less a museum with scores of Picassos and Braques and Chagalls. And the fine arts museum is only one of dozens of museums; and besides that, they have all that luscious chocolate! Rockford should be so lucky.

...... Well, there were further adventures, a visit to a paper mill and a great old cathedral with crypts and dead Swiss and everything, and a visit inevitably to a chocolate shop where I nearly bought a set of barbells but I remembered to speak French at the last moment so I walked away with a candy rabbit. And it rained the whole time, and I infer that such is the typical weather because these Baselians/Baseleens all walk around with umbrellas and there were numerous baby carriages covered with transparent plastic and mothers blithely chauffeuring about their young charges in the rain. But I have talked your ear off already, so I will just say *Auf Wiedersehen* which I think is German for "Watch your toes."

Ireland

Dublin and Surroundings

Winter blues and blahs were grinding gulleys in our souls, so Ellen and I thought we'd dash away for a sunlit week in the Caribbean. The first thing my Internet software travel agent site brought up to my screen, however, was not the Caribbean. It was a great deal on a weekend getaway to Ireland. Roundtrip from Chicago to Dublin was the price of a ticket to Kansas City. Too good to resist.

A week later we found ourselves skimming over the Atlantic and bound for the Emerald Isle. It was the tail-end of February, though, and we suspected it would be more of a Drab Brown Isle. But the flight was a breeze. We had, according to the pilot, a tail wind of nearly one hundred eight-five mph, and sure enough, in just about six hours we landed in Dublin.

It was raining as we slogged out of the airport to the bus stop, and we were to learn soon that in Ireland that time of year it rains every day. The rain patters down for fifteen minutes or half an hour. Then it disappears and the sun streams down for a few hours. The chill slanting rain comes again, then maybe a mist. And so on, and so on. It's not so bad, really, you just have to get used to it. And you learn to appreciate now and then a warming slug of Irish whiskey.

The bus shuttle from the airport to our lodgings south of Dublin had a name, as things tend to do in Ireland. It was called the Patton Flyer, and it made pretty good time to the suburb south of Dublin called Dun Laoghaire (pronounced dun-LEERY). The bus took us past scores of cranes in Dublin proper and down at the harbor, evidence of the impressive building boom going on in Ireland. As the passing scenery grew more suburban, we spotted daffodils in bloom, and then later we saw dogwood blossoms and redbud trees in pink silhouette. Back in Chicago, spring was still two months away, but in Dublin it was peeping from under rocks and ready to pounce on us.

Dun Laoghaire Fountain

The bus dumped us in downtown Dun Laoghaire, and we trundled our bags uphill to our bed and breakfast place. It had a name too – Ferry House – because it was located near the shore of the Irish Sea (Atlantic Ocean to you lubbers), and presumably near a ferry dock. The B&B was a nice old

Georgian home with high ceilings adorned with plaster gewgaws and a tiny bathroom built into our bedroom, and a community breakfast nook in the basement and a cheerful, talkative Irish family as hosts. We admired the ceiling and smiled at the homely paintings on the walls, and then we plopped into bed and took a long nap. Overnight to Ireland and losing six hours of darkness and skipping a night's sleep may fool some people – but it didn't fool my old bones for a minute. They wanted some sleep on Thursday night, and even though it was Friday morning they we going to have some of that sleep, by gum!

We emerged from the Ferry House when it was still morning and ambled about Dun Laoghaire. It had upscale boutique-like shops in the little downtown area, and we strolled along an elevated pathway at the sea shore, passing a tidy park with a long boat nestled in a bed of primroses. The boat was a giant planter, brimming with pansies and primroses and other blooms. As we neared the sea shore we were buffeted by stiff gusts of wind. A small child, just barely a toddler, was leaning into the wind, battling to take a step and giggling like crazy.

James Joyce Tower

We passed a flower shop with a catchy name: Bloomsday

Flowers. And that reminded me that we were in James Joyce's old haunts, and in fact the opening of his great novel Ulysses was set right here in Dun Laoghaire. We asked around and finally found a bit further south along the shore an old Martello tower, a round squat stone tower at water's edge, which now serves as the James Joyce Museum. We discovered that the museum was closed now, in the off-season, but that it would open for two hours on Saturday. But we could peer over the cliff edge at the foot of the tower and see the tide pools and the surf crashing against boulders not far from shore. It was exactly the scene at the opening of Ulysses, where the young protagonist Stephen Daedalus raises his shaving bowl to the heavens and lofts a prayer to the muses, a fitting parody and homage to the opening of Homer's great poem.

We walked down to water's edge. A sign there said something about protecting Irish seals. We saw a crow with a gray patch on its back, and I was reminded of a similar bird I saw in Egypt, and how I asked the Egyptian guide what they called those birds shaped like crows with the gray splotch, and she said, "We call those crows."

Ellen paused to snap pictures of the crow and I wandered down to an area marked off for bathing. I turned a corner behind slab of gray black rock and there, stepping out of the water stood a skinny white-haired man stark naked. He wrapped a towel around himself. Further down the beach I saw another fellow about ankle deep in the waves and also naked as a jaybird. I went back around the rock that hid the beach and suggested to Ellen that we head back to our inn. Later in chatting about the museum and that beach with our host's daughter Leann (her parents were called out of town, so the daughter made up our room and cooked us breakfast), she told us that the stretch of beach down there is a bit peculiar because it is still considered a "man's beach" and that some men insist on their right to go nude bathing there. It is also the place where local bloods gather on Christmas morning to plunge into the icy waters of the Irish Sea – to prove that they are manly (and that they are crazy or drunk or both).

Eager to get going with the sight-seeing, we boarded the DART (Dublin Area Rapid Transit) and zoomed back to town. Once again we passed scores of those Swedish cranes that look like lop-sided crosses made from a giant erector set. Everywhere we looked in Dublin gave evidence of a building craze. We alit at Tara Street Station, proceeded a block north to the Liffey River, wound through twisty streets, chic shops, assorted pubs and a pedestrian tunnel along Fleet Street until we emerged in the Temple Bar area. This is the equivalent of Rush Street back home, a trendy, over-priced, loud and lusty part of the city. A lot of drinking goes on in the Temple Bar area, and in fact the Dubliners refer to it as Temple Barf.

I was famished. We had been eating lightly, following a special diet Ellen got from the NASA web site, the Jet-Lag

105

diet it is called, with a regimen of feasting one day and fasting the next and thereby altering one's biological clock. It seemed to work, and we neither suffered much jet-lag, but on arrival it made me hungry enough to gnaw on my suitcase. We stopped at a coffee shop that turned out to be a creperie and we shared an apple pancake. The coffee was just average, but Ellen said the tea was excellent.

We did some window shopping but hesitated to buy. The prices of nearly everything seemed awfully high, and of course the dollar does not go far when translated into Euros. I had been in England a year or two ago, and I was used to the pound being worth two dollars. But the Euro! The Euro, which only last year when we visited Italy was about a dollar was now worth much more. A US dollar today only gets you a fraction of a Euro. Alas, America, we have sunk so far and fast in the world's economy that it makes the head spin. Or maybe we have risen like a rocket (compared to some currencies). Money makes the world go 'round the bend.

Book of Kells

Nearly the first thing that Ellen wanted to see was the Book of Kells. Ah, how can you resist a word-girl, an ex-English–major and bibliophile! I wasn't quite sure what was in the Book of Kells, but I thought it worth a look. We walked from a quaint shopping mall, sporting a fruit stand in the middle, to Trinity College in the heart of Dublin. The college presented what you might expect of an old European university: gray stone buildings vaguely gothic, swaths of green grass dotted with students toting backpacks, a few spires, glass-fronted administration buildings, and forlorn statues of men in robes gazing stonily at the raucous future. We ducked into a handsome sienna stone building that we thought might be the library where they housed the B-of-K, but no, it turned out to be the city's Natural History Museum --- or as they call it in Dublin, the Dead Zoo. Ellen got her picture taken standing in front of a petrified skeleton of a now-extinct Irish deer that was easily 12-feet tall.

We found the library/museum, paid our 12 Euros and joined a queue to enter the display areas. The Book of Kells, it turns out, is not one book but rather a collection of several elaborately illustrated books of the New Testament. Back in the days before printing presses, books were hand-lettered by platoons of tireless monks toiling in dank monasteries. One such bible factory was on the Scottish island of Iona, and the fruit of the monks' labors, some "illuminated" or embellished texts, ended up in the newly Christianized town of Kells, Ireland. The books were produced around 1000 C.E. and they had a checkered history for the next thousand years, once being stolen by those rascally invading Norwegians, hidden, buried for several weeks and eventually recovered and restored to the church.

The Book of Kells comes down to us as one of the most extraordinary art works of the Dark Ages because they were so elaborately illustrated. They consist of commonplace Latin text of the Bible, nice script of course but nothing special unless you're crazy about calligraphy. But most pages are adorned with colorful drawings – the first letter of a chapter often adorned with one or more fabulous drawings – of Medieval life scenes, hunting and cooking and dancing, or Celtic knots made of strange Irish mythic symbols like entwined serpents and three-headed birds. The illustrations get weirder and weirder the more you study them. The colors, even after a thousand years and even in the dim museum light, are bold and lively. They used real gold leaf on some pages and crushed lapis lazuli for deep blue and a paste of spider eggs to get a bright crimson. And the shapes are haunting and not quite like any other art style. The anonymous Irish artists of the Middle Ages produced stylized figures of Jesus and the Saints that resemble, at least in spirit, the figures on ancient Egyptian temples. One detail I noticed is that the beards of Jesus and John and others, the honored figures, have a patch cut out of the beard that reveals the man's chin. At first I thought it was the mouth, but then I saw that the mouth was higher and this was an ornament, a hole in the beard, that must have been the height of fashion in the Eleventh Century. The eyes were always facing us head-on, no matter if the head was turned, like an Egyptian pharaoh's eyes. Human figures are usually presented in a setting crammed with arcane symbols – a sword to represent power or a flower for chastity or a lamb to remind us of God's sacrifice.

All in all, the B-of-K was a fascinating glimpse into the past. They say that the book contains lapses and misspelling and errors, and that it was probably not meant for reading but rather served as stupendous holy object – a gorgeous thing to place on the altar in the Church to impress the illiterate peasants who entered the House of God. Much of the meaning is lost to all but the scholars, no doubt, but all of us can still marvel at the intricacy of its patterns and see the immensity of labor that went into its production, and possibly feel the intensity of it as an act of worship. It must have taken hundreds of monks over several generations to create the object. It was a book created by people who felt they were on the brink of eternal life. Another link, for me, with Egyptian culture, that patience, that vision of eternal life. They had all the time in the world.

After we quitted the room where they housed the B-of-K, we followed a hand-lettered sign to a place called the Long Room in another part of the Trinity College Library. At the top of a dusty stairway, we entered a huge vaulted library reading room. The room was easily thirty feet high and fifty feet deep, and it was crammed floor to ceiling with books. The books seemed ancient and quietly mysterious. Battered leather covers were falling off some shelves and some books were tied together with twine. Room decoration consisted of marble busts of ancient scribes – Petrarch and Dante and

Homer. Long ladders stretched from the worn wooden floors to the high shelves looming overhead. The whole place smelled of must and crumbling paper. It was like strolling the set from a Harry Potter movie.

At the museum shop just before the exit, Ellen found a Christmas tree ornament bearing an intricate Celtic knot. I bought an Irish tin whistle. From the back of the shop wafted soft lilting speech, not exactly folk songs, but then not exactly mere conversation. It was the everyday speech of the island Jonathan Swift called "a land of poets and slaves." The speech made me want to break into brogue. Aye, faith, begorrah and shiver me timbers! [I always get my Irishmen and pirates mixed up.]

England

London

During a long-term work assignment in England, I lived variously in London, Manchester, Basingstoke and again in London. I kept notes. There was time for weekend jaunts to the countryside and a few holidays with longer stays at familiar tourist attractions. Common language, customs and climate make England the most comfortable destination in Europe. Here follows an account of some travels in "jolly olde England."

London was larger than New York but pleasantly quieter. My hotel in lay in the shadow of St Paul's Cathedral in the financial district of west London. From my room I looked east to see a charming 18th Century guildhall, Stationer's Hall, and beyond that a massive gray ovoid stretching into a gray sky, the dome of St. Paul's. For my morning stroll I headed to the little courtyard between my businessman's hotel, the Club Quarters, and Stationer's Hall. Like so much of London, the area was jam-packed with history. A plaque on the stone wall stated that on this spot in 15-something, one Wyndym de Worde (yep, that's the fellow's real name), the "Father of Fleet Street," set up his printing shop. According to my guidebook, the location was logical for a printer because it was near St Paul's Churchyard, an area of the city that has been a nexus of booksellers for centuries, even before printing was introduced to England by William Caxton in 14-something-else. For we bookish, English-speaking folks, London serves as Mecca, and we are forever on pilgrimage.

Last night wandering Fleet Street before stopping in the Tipperary for a steak pie and bitters, I stumbled upon Dr Samuel Johnson's house. It has been preserved pretty much intact as an example of 18th Century residences, a squat brick building with ornate chimney and narrow staircases. Today it serves as a small museum to the man who wrote the first English dictionary. I had toured the house on a previous trip to London, but this time it made more sense, in that it was located on a crooked lane leading just off Fleet Street, the center of the newspaper business in 18th Century London. For a time, the prolific Doctor Johnson wrote for a rag-tag London newspaper, the Spectator I believe, while he was working on his monumental dictionary. Johnson was my favorite late 18th Century character, not only because he compiled the first English dictionary – and became the first (and greatest) editor of Shakespeare's works – and invented literary biography and criticism in Lives of the Poets – but also because he was a tease, a scholar, a curmudgeon and a brilliant conversationalist, as revealed in Boswell's irreplaceable biography. He must have been also a lonely man. He left all his worldly possessions to black manservant, Francis Barber.

By the time I found Johnson's museum this trip, it was 10 p.m. and the place was closed Just outside the handsome 200-yr-old brick residence, two workmen were hip deep in a hole, repairing power lines. One of them looked up as I passed and said, "Gud evenin', gov'nor," and I felt like I had just stepped through the gravedigger's scene in <u>Hamlet</u>.

Very early yesterday morning – it was 5:30 am or so, and about midnight biological time – I checked out the route to my office, just a few doors up Ludgate Hill and nearly opposite St Paul's Cathedral. Mistaking my way back, I stepped into a private lane, a cul-de-sac as it turned out, because the far end was blocked by a locked wrought-iron gate. The lane led to a moss-covered square and a row of smart orange brick houses or apartments with a small English garden in the center. It was a residential enclave, here in the heart of London. Through a huge picture window, I saw a couple sipping tea at the breakfast table. A little further on was a child's wooden swing set, complete with climbing rope and ladder. On all sides were neatly planted flower boxes holding large lustrous yellow pansies. On the grounds I found geraniums and irises in bloom, here in early February. A child and mother emerged from a blue door in the orange brick wall and proceeded to walk hand-in-hand toward the busy city street. Strolling back to the main street, Paternoster Row, where my office is located, and just past Ave Maria Lane I found yet another helpful sign declaring that the tiny oasis I had visited was "Amen Corner". The entrance was festooned with small plastic plaques declaring that Amen Corner had been awarded for the last six years running an honorable mention from the London Gardeners Association. I stared up at the cathedral dome and thought, aha, Amen Corner, Ave Maria Lane and Paternoster Row... okay, okay London, I get it.

Friday morning 3 a.m. and I guess I am still suffering from jet lag. I went to sleep all right about 10:30, after a very pleasant dinner with my new friend, John, and a few glasses of excellent wine, and I snagged three or four hours sleep. Then I awoke bleary-eyed but restless to stumble into walking clothes – my jeans, black sweatshirt, rubber-soled shoes and sports jacket – and headed into the London air.

Modern London is not like the old Sherlock Holmes movies, at least not what I've seen so far. No thick fog and enshrouded alleys and madmen lurking in stairways. The city is well-lit, generally kempt and, at 3 a.m. pleasantly quiet. I heard the bells of St Paul's strike the quarter-hour. Traffic was sparse, but there, both foot and automobile. The few policemen I saw looked more like puttering gardeners than stalkers of Mr. Hyde.

I meandered down Ludgate Hill and turned north on Old Bailey, aiming for St. Bartholomew's Hospital. My friend Mary had been a nurse in training there, and I thought it would be amusing to see her old haunts. After a few blocks I spied a huge open-air structure, massive gray walls topped by a high glass roof like a train station. It reminded me a little of Waterloo Station, in fact, where I caught a train this morning – make that Thursday morning, in order to visit a client in suburban Basingstoke. As I approached the building, I noticed that it was brightly lighted and alive with shouting men in white coats. I thought they must be doctors streaming from ward to ward. Outside the building stood scores or hundreds of white trucks, and in my colossal ignorance I thought they were ambulances sufficient to haul an army of sick and wounded up to the hospital gates. What could be happening that would bring out an army medical corps in the dead middle of London at three a.m.? It must be a tsunami coming, I thought, a great rip in the floor of the North Sea, to be followed soon by a wall of water high enough to drown Big Ben. Then I read the signage on the trucks: Forbes Poultry, Myer's Lamb and Beef, Tidwell and Sons Sausage.

Smith's Meat Market

I had blundered upon the central London meat market, Smith's Meat Market, and at 3 a.m. now abuzz at the height of activity. Men in white butcher's coats (and I saw now also wearing hardhats and goggles) were hauling carts of animal carcasses and freshly packaged chops and steaks up and down great aisles of butcher counters. The huge marketplace bristled with butchers and meat mongers, a hubbub of clanging hand trolleys, chatter, rattling carts and rude shouts. One aisle was apparently reserved for retail trade and I strolled past hundreds of beef carcasses -- pig hoofs and heads and whatall, tubs of beef tongues, trays gleaming with livers, gizzards, brains and assorted bloody

115

organs. A dozen or so patrons – perhaps professional chefs seeking the perfect boar's head or fillet mignon – argued with the butchers and prodded thick slabs of meat and bobbed here and there among the forest of animal parts. After a few minutes gazing at the carnage I felt a need for fresh air.

Back on the street, I turned past a small park or garden area, crossed a narrow lane and abruptly halted before another large graystone building complex: St Bart's Hospital. The institution presented a modest, if not downright homely facade with formidable, massive walls, but graced at the back by what must be a chapel in which stained glass windows glowed like living rainbows thrust into the dark night air. Continuing along the walkway I passed the Henry VIII gate, then passed the Nurses' Gate, and I imagined Mary as a young woman in starched cap scurrying into that doorway, a bit breathless and late for class, or else giggling at what a girl classmate said about the old gent with the scrofula. It's odd, isn't it, how we can reconstruct a life with just a few scraps of information, like an anthropologist reconstructing a Neanderthal face from a cheekbone fragment and a bicuspid.

Across from the Nurses Gate was yet another road sign that read "School of Nursing and Midwifery" and below that a sign which read "Butchers Hall". About a hundred cornball jokes popped into my head, relating the nearby meat market to the hospital surgery, but I quickly shook them out of my head. It was a joke no doubt that had been done to death.

Headed back toward the hotel, I passed the General Post Office. An inscription on the keystone announced that King Edward VI laid the stone which became the foundation for modern British postal service, and that he was "pretty damn proud of himself" (or words to that effect). I might have slid past the post office without noticing it except that I paused to ponder a statue of a solemn man in a frock coat, one Rowland Hines, who created the first modern postage stamp in 1840. Before his time, I suppose, there was no glue on the back of stamps and they kept falling off.

Almost home now, I paused once again to admire St Paul's Cathedral. Lights out at 4 a.m. and the great dome not so resplendent now, but somehow more imposing. What a lot of hay you could put in St Paul's Cathedral! And they say that it was built on the site of an even larger Norman cathedral dating back to medieval times but destroyed in the Great Fire of London in 1666. The back of the cathedral was still dark and the weather-stained back entrance provided a startling contrast to the noble gray, recently sand-blasted front. One speculates that it would take a million pigeons a million years to produce that particular shade of green-gray.

At the front of St Paul's stands a statue complex, a woman on a pedestal thirty feet high. She is marble but she is holding a scepter and orb of brass. The inscription says the statue is a replica of an earlier statue of Queen Anne. The replica was erected in 1889. I think to myself, for crying out loud, in London they not only have history, but they are refurbishing it, just about the time we Americans begin creating a bit of our own. Our memorials seem paltry compared to their history of centuries and the march of empire. They have ancient kings and timeless myths. Americans must make do with quaint tourist advisories: "On this site in 1723, a Mountain Man killed a skunk" or perhaps "Here, in the year of our Lord 1899, a pioneer peed".

At the base of the Queen Anne statue sit four marble women. One holds a brass trident, one a brass bow, one a tambourine and one a lyre. I am not sure what they are supposed to represent, but I notice that they are all bare-breasted. And maybe that is the point. The object of displaying bare-breasted women is to display bare-breasted women.

Friday night I went to dinner with my U.K. manager, D. and his wife. My boss and I dotted some "i's" and crossed a few "t's" at the office and then rushed out to catch a nearby subway train (the "Tube") for Piccadilly. We emerged from the underground horde into a larger and rowdier above-ground horde. The scene was vibrant: Londoners in a party mood, businessmen in dark suits, girl punk rockers in stiletto heels and leather pants, dazed Koreans and Indians looking even more lost than me, working class guys in soccer sweatshirts and Chicago Bulls caps, a winding, jostling, talkative and possibly tipsy crowd. We met the wife on a busy corner and walked north almost into Soho before we ducked into a pub. Like most English watering holes, right after the work day it roared with talk and laughter and clattering glassware. We swept upstairs to a slightly quieter and definitely less smoky dining area. The ale was good, but the fish and chips second-rate.

Our conversation drifted pleasantly, but it kept turning to the difficulties of London life. My American friends moved to London with their four children from a big house in a small town near Chicago, just north of the Wisconsin border. They seemed a little harried by it all, and no wonder, having to place their kids in private "American" schools (at $18,000 per annum per kid) and take a much smaller house an awkward distance from London at triple the price of their comfortable American home. And the people were helpful but alien, and the food dubious, and the driving difficult (more on that later), and the prices sky-high. They. said they had quit trying to figure out the price of things in US dollars, because it was too discouraging. They just thought of prices in pounds, and gritted their teeth in the Tasco grocery store.

I got to thinking that my friends were pretty typical of American ex-patriots, the very sort of people whom large corporations send overseas, bright, energetic, and clueless. They are not philistines, exactly, not brutal or brash, but rather hard working and sincere and, well, both unprepared and unimaginative. Largely consumed with making their way in the USA, they rose quickly in corporate America, were successful, affluent, and mobile – so mobile that they came to mind for an assignment overseas. However, they were not scholars, not adventurers. They were the kind of people who think of Shakespeare as boring, and museums as places to take the children, and the House of York as a brand of shoe.

So they get plunked down in England and they don't have a very good time. Their house is not as nice as their American house. It lacks good central heating and their furniture won't fit. They got a plum assignment, but it wasn't quite what they expected and so they spend time and money keeping the foreign country at arm's length. They begin to pay extra for American foods, American clothes, American movies. They send their kids to "American" schools (which nowadays are half filled with Indians and Indonesians), and they befriend those near at hand, other Americans, and the wife joins a Wives Club where American women form coffee-hour committees and entertain each other complaining about prices, their husband's new-found urge to drink too much, and the snobby English. They seem like the very sort of people who get sent overseas, and who largely represent America to Europeans, and the sort that Europeans quickly begin to resent. Two of the Englishmen I have met over here waxed eloquent (after the third glass of wine) and made sweeping statements about "how Americans are". One said that Americans have no sense of irony (even though he quoted Mark Twain to me). And the other said that Americans have such a large and rich country that they cannot really understand people who live highly confined lives, or lives filled with constant struggle. When I heard those comments I thought they were misguided – how could they ignore the struggles of pioneer people who wrested civilization from a raw and lonely continent -- how could they miss the irony in a nation that outlawed liquor and then bathed in booze? But now I think I see where they come from. They might have been describing my practical and parochial friends. They had simply never met the kind of Americans I left back home.

Covent Garden

After I left my friends in Leicester (pronounced "Lester") Square, I wandered a bit. The town seems to me rich and old, like Cleopatra in the Bard's phrase "Age cannot wither her, nor custom stale her infinite variety." But London isn't all that complicated. Ten minutes stroll took me past the movie houses (cinema or Odeon) and into Soho, which used to be the "sin" section of London but today resembles a pretty tame sidewalk masquerade party. Ten minutes more and I had wandered down to Trafalgar Square to admire the gigantic sculpted lions and the lighted tip of Big Ben and to gawk at a gorgeous Degas exhibit at the National Gallery, and another five minutes' walk led to Covent Garden, a large open- air flea market ringed by good restaurants and night clubs. The upper floor sports a hundred interesting boutiques and a section of folding tables where independent merchants sell woolens, handmade jewelry, knickknacks and everything under the sun. The lower floor houses more shops, more restaurants, including an Italian *al fresco* place where people gather to see the free entertainment – jugglers, magicians and such. The regular entertainment had just ended when a young woman in blue jeans stepped forward, placed a tape recorder on the floor, cranked it up to full volume for accompaniment and proceeded to belt out arias from La Traviata, Carmen and other golden-oldies. She had a decent voice, and the crowd seemed to appreciate her combination of singing skill and chutzpah. I may have dropped a pound in the hat myself.

Leaving the one-man-band operetta brought me to a severe disappointment. I had gone to Covent Garden in search of a particular shop, a museum really, that I had chanced upon during my first visit to London. It was a museum or showplace devoted to ingenious wooden toys, designed by a minor genius named Eric Stolz. He was a showman who built and sold hand-cranked wooden curios full of wooden gears, hand-carved cogs, and mechanical movements clever as a cuckoo clock. He made intricately hinged dinosaurs and dancing girls and yawning lions. For me, it was love at first sight.

But the museum was gone. In its place was a rather ordinary toy store that held finger puppets and yo-yos and glossy backgammon games. Alas, the American Bard laments, "Nothing gold can stay." At one point I left in disgust, but I returned to have a torturous conversation with the (French) proprietress, who eventually understood what I wanted and pointed me to the very rear of the place where I discovered a dusty shelf that held half a dozen kits designed by Eric Stolz himself. I glommed a kit for a wooden drummer. You turn the handle and his foot goes up and down working a wooden cymbal, his hands fly up and down thumping a wooden drum set and his head wags side to side. To this middle-aged boy-at-heart, such finds are part of the joy of tourism. I left clutching my treasure and humming a hip-hip-hoorah for Covent Garden.

Bloomsbury

Saturday morning began with café latte and an odd but tasty cream cheese and pimento wrap outside the Tube station. And then, shaazham! Off to Bloomsbury. The section of London known as Bloomsbury is a favorite haunt of mine because, being a bookish fellow, I like to rub shoulders with all the famous writers who have lived there. In the early 20th century the neighborhood could boast a clique of painters, writers and other intellectuals known as the Bloomsbury Circle – Virginia and Leonard Wolfe, E.M. Forster and a herd of wanna-bes. One of the magnets of the neighborhood has got to be the British Museum – where I will drop in later – but my first stop: Charles Dickens' House.

Dickens banged about various sites in London before he became a household word and bought an impressive estate on the outskirts. His place in Bloomsbury was a home he acquired in his first prosperity, after Pickwick Papers became a big hit, and there he wrote three or four novels – the most popular being Oliver Twist. The house is nicely preserved on an upscale middle-class boulevard. Bright brass knocker on the bright green door which one must bang for admittance, and pay four pounds to a chipper and yet reserved lady in grey who dismisses one with "Oh, just wander where you will, but don't skip the third floor".

Being an middle class male and a four-time home-owner, I headed immediately for the basement. There was no plant to see – no furnace, no fuse box, no plumbing worth mentioning. Instead there was a small study – probably in Dickens' time a children's room – lined with chairs and at the far end a large screen t-v. Politely I watched a cycling video recapitulating Dickens' busy life, his birth in a small rural town and family's move to the great city where his father found odd work for a time but not enough to support his lofty tastes, so that in time he was slung into debtor's prison. The boy Charles Dickens was put to work in a boot blacking factory, an odious and humiliating experience which was to work its way subtly into nearly all the novels. Then the young man began to walk the town in his first job as a journalist, and he amused his friends and eventually his readers with imaginative stories about bumbling, amiable characters, and a publisher asked him to turn the stories into a book, and so on, and so on…. I left the video early, having read the book.

Around the corner was a doorway open to a small garden a half-story below sidewalk level. To one side of the garden stood a locked grating and visible through the grating one saw stacks of wine bottles. The Dickens wine cellar, then, was open air, but securely locked. Dusty purple bottles softly gleamed in the shadows. A dozen bottles of French burgundy, of course, and maybe a nice claret too.

The main floor of the house consisted of a kitchen at the back (where the volunteers were collecting entrance fees and distributing pamphlets), and a living room lined with paintings of C.D., his family and friends, various landscapes of the English countryside, and a sitting room at the front of the house furnished with glass stands full of family bric-a-brac: a cigar cutter, a feathered hat of Mrs. Dickens, some crockery, an ornate grandfather clock. Ho hum. Some of the notes from family friends remark on the frail health or weariness of Dickens' wife, and apparently friends reckoned that he was running her and the children ragged. More than one of his biographers comments on his astonishing energy, the busiest, hardest working and hardest playing man they had ever met.

Upstairs, the second-floor bedrooms had been transformed into small museums. More portraits and some sly caricatures of Dickens and friends, a few sticks of furniture, and at the back of the house the best room, the Master's study, with a sunny big window bathing in soft morning light his writing desk. The desk held a few quill pens, a tray to hold the powdery sand used to dry ink, and a nice touch -- a ceramic monkey. Apparently, Dickens always had to have that monkey on his writing desk, as a paperweight perhaps, or maybe a good luck charm.

The third-floor rooms introduced a period of Dickens' life that I had never understood very well. It was crammed with posters announcing his public readings, and the walls were hung with framed maps, receipts, and hotel arrangements that detailed his assistant's plan for Dickens' travels. I knew that toward the end of his life Dickens began reading his works in public. I learned now that he had always nourished a love of theatre, and that in fact he wrote and acted in several amateur theatricals. At first, he had read in public as a way to raise money for charities. Given his novels of moral outrage and scathing social criticism, he was always being asked to help a good cause. And then occasionally, inevitably, he needed the money himself. Although a fabulously well-off writer, Dickens was perpetually looking for money because he spent the stuff faster than it could be printed. His publisher suggested a few readings, to publicize his latest books and to fill the Dickens coffers, and the readings were a smash.

In a sense, Charles Dickens was the first literary superstar. People from all over Europe thronged to see him, and he put on a great show. His notes indicate where he planned to insert a dramatic pause, where a sweeping gesture. His audiences wept at the death of Little Nell, and shuddered when Bill Sikes set off to commit murder. His tour of the United States was everywhere standing-room-only, and there were letters to the editor in Chicago complaining that people "of the first quality" were turned away.

Although his doctors warned him against the great strain of the tours – and although he took, according to his diary, a raw egg in a glass of brandy three times a day to keep up his strength, finally he collapsed during a performance. He seems to have been mildly obsessed by the drama and adulation of the readings, and he wanted to go on again. But he cancelled his last tour, returned to England, and died a year later. It came home to me that Dickens – a genius of course, a man of remarkable wit and vitality, a fellow who achieved a sort of immortality through his books -- nonetheless needed that audience adulation. All his life a part of him remained the little boot black with something to prove.

Lunch was a nice lemon chicken risotto with a glass of pinot noir. I find myself drinking (alcohol) more in England than ever in my life. These folks drink morning noon and night. The habit slips on as easily as a good old shoe.

British Museum

Off to the British Museum, just a few blocks from Dickens home and museum. I love the noble entryway, the stately columns, the crowds in the gigantic reading room (and love the idea that a museum, replete with curios and artifacts from around the world, should offer at its heart a collection of books, a chance to delve more deeply into the matters presented in the specimen cases). My plan was to skip the obvious attractions – the Parthenon fragments, the Rosetta Stone – since "been there, done that." I had a suspicion that I would be driving out to Salisbury Plain one of these weekends to see Stonehenge, and I wanted to snoop around the display on early human inhabitants of the British Isles.

People have been around a long time, and before the Roman conquest – which was long before the Angles and Saxons and what we think of as ancient Britain – there were people on those islands, planting crops, building cities, swapping wives, stealing cattle and all the things that make for civilization. The early folks were Bronze Age people (and of course the Romans were an Iron Age civilization that ran through the natives like a knife through butter). The early inhabitants built huts and made boats and raised pigs. Their villages tended to be small, but stable. They probably learned to make clothing stuffed with dry grass to provide a layer of insulation, Bronze Age Gore-tex. They worshipped gods and had priests (Druids). They buried their dead, sometimes with worldly goods, sometimes without.

The museum cases held pottery, amber jewelry and crude bronze tools. The case that fired my imagination was a stash of spear heads, all bent and gnarled as though they were hastily and a bit belatedly retrieved from a fire. The historical tidbit printed on a card beside the bronze spearheads is something that will stay with me a while. It noted that caches of bronze weapons have been unearthed all over the British Isles. Sometimes they come from graves, sometimes woodland, but most often they are found near marshes and riverbanks, places that the pre-historic peoples considered magical or holy. And once in a while the cache of weapons is found to be deformed -- just like the ones in the case -- half melted, or pounded into a misshapen and useless bronze clod. And I wondered about that recurring phenomenon. The display case gave no explanation – just the bare fact that ancient weapons turn up that way, buried perhaps a thousand years apart. It makes me think that perhaps ancient man from time to time grew disgusted with war. For generations, perhaps in some remote valley, one tribe attacked another. We steal your sheep, you steal ours; you rape our women, we rape yours; you kill us, we kill you, and there's no end to it. And then I imagine a meeting, dawn in a meadow, where the warriors of the two tribes come together and decide, in effect, that "we ain't gonna study war no more." They build a great fire and throw all their spearpoints and swords and arrowheads in it, and when the metal had softened they beat it into a lump. Then they bury the hatchet, literally, or else throw it in some sacred swamp. They walk away in peace. For a while.

All this happened time and again – beginning at least 5000 years ago. The roar of war is in the heart of man. And so too is the song of peace.

By the time I decompressed culturally and staggered out of the British Museum for the London streets, it was dark and chilly. My feet hurt and my eyes burned. I stopped in a pub for a quick pint and a bite. The dish on the menu sounded like authentic English fare: Toad in a Hole. This turned out to be a bowl made of flakey pastry (the hole) filled with two sausages (the toad) and slathered with stewed onions. Not bad, actually, especially with a pint of bitters.

Piccadilly Circus

After a brief ride on the Tube I made it to Piccadilly Circus just in time for the 8 o'clock show at the Criterion Theatre. It was something recommended by my American friends, as a London theatrical treat (and not too expensive). The show was called "The Complete Works of William Shakespeare (Abridged)" and it turned out to be the farce the title suggests. This suited me fine, since I was pretty tired and in a mood for cheap laughs. However, the show was silly, occasionally rising to cleverness, but mostly disappointing because it featured three Americans doing burlesque sendups of Shakespeare. Who needs more Americans for crying out loud – and especially Americans doing poopoo jokes at the Bard's expense? If this stuff tickles the English, they must possess a sixth-grader sense of humor. Of course, now that I think it of it, the audience consisted mostly of German high school students on a field trip. They were so excited and shot up with hormones that they would giggle at the wallpaper. I left the theatre slightly groggy and caught the Tube back to my hotel. In the dark as I strolled past St

Paul's Cathedral, I spied a pedestal on the church grounds that I had passed hurriedly before. But this time I paused to read the inscription. For those who value eloquence, I send it along verbatim. It was inscribed in a spiral script, so that you walk around and around the pedestal to read:

In war, resolution
In defeat, defiance
In victory, magnanimity
In peace, good will
1939-1945
Remember before God the People of London

Drive on the Left You Fool

Driving an automobile in England is a sort of vast topological riddle, seemingly simple but devilishly sly, designed to exalt the humble and to shame the seeming-wise. I gave my love a cherry, it had no stone.

To begin with, of course, they drive on the left. At first the change seems daunting, barreling down the highway in the lane reserved for oncoming traffic, but very quickly the difference disappears and even we left-handers, notoriously befuddled by the flip-flop of near-instinctual strong hand orientation, adapt to the left lane mentality. Oh, we may have an anxious moment or two when we first attempt a turnaround in a narrow city lane, turning hard left into a clogged alley, then reversing, yikes, across the right lane to the left before slamming it into first gear and proceeding back whence we came and look out for approaching cars because they bear down on us not in the passing lane but on their right-of-way, the left. Unnerving occasionally, yes, but easy once you get the hang of it. After a day or two it begins to seem even, in a left-handed way, logical.

The cars are mirror images of real cars. Driver sits on the right side, shotgun on his or her left. The gearshift is managed with the left hand, the wipers where the lights should be and the lights where you reach for the wipers. It had been, what, twelve years since I had driven a stick shift, but the skills came back quickly. A little awkward, though, reaching for the stick with the right hand and bumping into the door handle, then reaching back with the left hand to encounter the stick, to downshift when I meant to upshift. Oddly enough, the feet are not reversed: left foot clutch, right foot brake and accelerator. A foolish consistency is the hobgoblin of little minds.

A road map of England looks like a spilled bucket of worms. Nary a straight line to be found, from Land's End to Scotland. Instead main roads meander around the countryside, here turning gracefully around a gently sloping hill, and there curving sharply around an abandoned buttermilk churn. And, as if pointless curves and squiggles of asphalt weren't inefficient enough, the roads were disrupted every few miles with traffic obstacles called "roundabouts".

A roundabout is the English equivalent of a traffic circle, a place along the highway where from two to seven roads intersect by pouring into a tight oval or circle of pavement, around which one drives in a clockwise direction until one in despair exits on one of the roads and proceeds to careen off in the wrong direction. Eventually one encounters another roundabout, and with great care and skill, one manages to whirl around that circle until one exits and zooms back to the original roundabout. This can go on for hours if not months, depending on the size of one's fuel tank.

The trouble with most roundabouts is that the signage is foreign to all but the local inhabitants – who never look at the signage anyway. One encounters a roundabout warning – a road sign sprouting an oval symbol with squid-like tentacles including one large tentacle labeled "London M3" 2 mi. This is clearly meant to indicate that at the next roundabout one will see a few negligible side paths followed by a large four-lane path marked "London M3 Thisaway". What one finds, however, upon approaching this whirlpool of traffic dotted with menacing steel hulks darting in front and behind one's vehicle, is a rapid succession of indifferent little exits, marked with pale, poorly lettered road signs: "Pudwinkle, Nestings and Bother Crawley", "Poololly This Waye", "We regret to Inform You that you Just Passed Buttermilk Churn", and "Not London You Bloody Yank". And so naturally and constantly one gets lost. One spends hours circling round and round these traffic loops, wondering whether Pudwinkle or Poololly is the proper route to London.

And finally, after learning to drive on the left, after mastering the vicious roundabout, one must drive into a petrol station for a fill-up. In all decency, the people who man the cash registers in petrol stations should wear masks. I didn't even attempt to settle my bill -- I just walked away and left the car there at the pump, figuring that the cost of a tankful of ethyl would just about balance nicely with the equity in the car, so that the folks at Ford England and British Petroleum could fight over the vehicle and leave me well out of it.

Eventually I made my way 40 miles or so southwest of London and settled in the modest Hilton Hotel in the burg of Basingstoke. This town is one of several small industrial cities ringing London and built up in the late forties when the City proper was still too torn up from The War for construction. The town eventually became home to a number of international firms, including the site of my client's European headquarters. It was to serve as my work sire and also as base camp for my sorties into the English countryside. After an afternoon contending with English traffic, all I wanted was a stiff drink, a warm bath, and to go to bed sucking my thumb.

Winchester

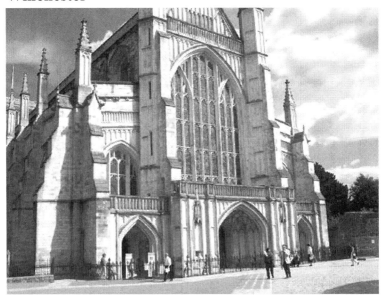

The drive Saturday morning took me past rolling hills of farmland and small villages. It was Hampshire countryside, but it might have been my homeland in southern Illinois, the neat green fields separated by stands of birch trees and sluggish streams dotted with willow and poplar. I took the roundabout that led up to Winchester and, small miracle, found the exit for town center first try and wended (wound?) my way to the multi-story parking lot. Parking in the snug little stalls was like trying to re-insert a sardine in a can of sardines.

By happy chance I had picked market day to visit Winchester, and so I emerged from the parking facility into a street lined with interesting market stalls and jammed with shoppers. The market was a hodge-podge of goods – rhubarb jam and piccalilli next to cell phones and pagers, quaint old Christmas wrapping papers next to a stall selling potted geraniums and fresh forced daffodil blooms. At the start of the day I had thought I might just stop by Winchester and then drive on to see Stonehenge in the afternoon, but once I had dawdled in the marketplace, I realized that it would be wise to spend the whole day in Winchester, tour the cathedral and soak up the atmosphere.

Winchester is a fine example, at least in my experience, of ancient English towns. It has been a populous place for more than two thousand years. A natural river port, it was a pre-Roman settlement on the Ichen river and then site of a big Roman fortification, and then, with the withdrawal of Rome, an important marketplace and religious site for the Anglo-Saxons. It was effectively the capitol of the country at one time, or at least it was the stronghold city in the 8th Century or so for King Alfred. In 1066 when the Normans took over England, they quickly moved to Winchester and built a great towering cathedral – partly no doubt as thanks to their God for victory, but also partly to cement their power by showing the populace that they had the biggest, baddest temple in the most important city in England. The cathedral, which today is treasured as a spiritual pinnacle and aesthetic wonder, the claim to fame of the pleasant ancient town, was at one time the nation's dominant political statement.

Winchester is closely packed, so that all the sights – the modern shopping area, the ancient castles, the cathedral and museums and all – are readily walkable. Just east of the old cobbled streets which teem with the Saturday morning market lie the modern shops, still narrow winding streets but now studded with pharmacies, department stores, Arpeggio and Bulgari and Calvin Klein. And just past the shops lies a large swath of greenery, a churchyard dotted with crypts and headstones and in the center of the park, huge and stately as an ocean liner, sits Winchester Cathedral.

Although the outside looks impressively large, the full scale of the place really hits home only from the inside. Passing through an ordinary house-sized doorway into a small reception area (3 pounds 50 donation, please) and then under a stone balcony to emerge in the nave, one looks up. The first view of the ceiling is awesome. It soars up, eighty or ninety feet high, achingly high like fireworks tapering into narrow graceful gothic arches.

The floor plan of Winchester Cathedral forms a cross. The long entryway passage, or nave, is the base of the cross. It ends at a large central circular area holding the altar, the main choir seating area and a massive screen made of carved stone. Beyond the screen lies another long passageway, the top of the cross, leading to chapels for ancient kings and for St. Mary. To the left of the altar another wing forms the perpendicular of the cross and leads to a chapel, a secluded place to pray, lined with painted wooden coffins, statuary and more saints' bones. To the right of the altar the final arm of the cross leads to still more specialty prayer spots, the library and a chapel to fishermen containing the gravestone of Izaak Walton, author of The Compleat Angler. All the walls are studded with carved stones commemorating the dead. Here a plaque with kind words for a long-gone king or counselor, there a bas-relief memorial to a general and a father and a neighbor, everywhere shield-sized stones set in the floor and walls, lettered with fond remembrances of church benefactors.

Just past the entrance is one grave-sized stone set in the floor where visitors linger. It is the grave marker for Jane Austen, the great 19th Century novelist. She had lived all her life in the neighborhood, at the village of Alton or Cawley about 10 miles distant. She was moved to Winchester during her last illness, and in fact she died just a stone's throw from the cathedral. She was only forty-one when she died. The gravestone announces that she was a friend who will be missed, the loving daughter of a local clergyman, a kind and devout soul. Nowhere does it mention that, oh yes, she also wrote books.

I pause a few moments near Jane Austen's stone. A few cathedral tourists pass by, and most study the grave marker and a couple even reach down to rub the stone words. One woman who has stooped to trace the dates with her fingers looks up with moist eyes and I imagine that, like me, she is savoring memories of the wonderfully simple, precise prose and gentle sensibility of Jane Austen. Our eyes catch and we exchange a swift smile of fellowship. Ah, we readers are such a sentimental lot!

I wander about the cathedral, gawking at the carved bishops of the great stone altar, snooping in alcoves that hold saints' bones, and pausing to light a candle or two for my children at a wax-encrusted genuflection stand. In the north wing, the left arm of the cross, I descend a curved stair to encounter the basement crypt, which the guide books tell me sometimes floods. Today it is dry and almost barren, holding only a single, stark statue of a man in prayer. Upstairs again, the choir area glows from candlelight on magnificent, intricately-carved wooden pews of dark mahogany. The altar itself holds the typical gaudy, gilded knickknacks of High Church. In fact, the whole cathedral is a collection of wooden effigies and musty coffins and bishops' diamond rings and similar doo-dads of Anglican religion. Climbing another marble stairway in the south wing, I reach the library.

One of the docents – or "volunteers" as she calls herself – seems to take an interest in me after I ask her why the style of the marble columns seems to change toward the back of the cathedral. She gives me a personal mini-tour, explaining that the older more stream-lined columns were erected over the Roman ruins in the 11th and 12th Centuries when the Normans had just taken power in England and needed to demonstrate their power and reverence to the subject Saxons. Later, in the 13th Century of so, the work was less hasty and the columns began to sport more carvings, more flowery and ornate capitals. The marble disks that were stacked to make the 80-foot high gothic arches are much smaller in the older columns, probably actually an indication of better engineering or masonry on the part of the earlier Norman builders. The older stones were a size that one man could carve and carry to the building site. The later stones were 2-3 times as large and would have required a team of men to carry and set in place. The volunteer also pointed to places in the walls that were repaired or patched, the result of "inferior" work by later builders – inferior in the sense that it only lasted 500 years before needing repairs. The volunteer was a townswoman and a member of the congregation.

The library held a small but choice collection of ancient books, mostly bibles and books of Common Prayer. It was begun before the widespread use of mechanical type, the result of a gift from one book collector (whose name escapes me) who donated hundreds of "illuminated" or hand-lettered texts. The pride of the library was the "Winchester Bible", a large two-foot by three-foot leather bound bible lavishly illustrated with ornate capital letters at the chapter headings and finely detailed pictures in the margins.

The illustrations had visibly different styles, indicating that the book resulted from a team of laborers (monks). One artist had a sort of Art Deco style where the folds of the Apostle's gowns swirled in precise fine lines over muscular legs and torsos. Another long-dead hand captured the folds in erratic thick and thin lines, with tiny cross-hatching for shading the fabric. Still another hand did the gothic lettering and still another applied the gold and lapis colors to the chapter headings. A single page of the foot-thick text must have taken a dozen monks many months to illustrate. Time was different in a 13th Century monastery. And they had no television.

As I was leaving the library, a guide noticed my American accent. The usual brief chat about Chicago: "Is it still full of gangsters and tommy-gun fire in the streets?" The polite but firm response: "Yes, but today they use AK-47s" The guide, like the volunteer who led me through the cathedral chapels, mentioned that America held two pages from the Winchester Bible in private collections. She seemed wistful as she remarked that "we truly could wish them restored to Winchester."

Just outside the cathedral I stopped for lunch at a combination gift shop and cafeteria. The food at The Refectory was fresh, a nice arugula and cucumber salad with a pot of tea. The lady in the serving line especially recommended what I thought was "laudy cake" – perhaps an especially praiseworthy pastry. I took a slice and then thought to ask her how one might spell the name of that dessert. She said, "It's laudy – l-a-r-d-y." Indeed, it turned out to be doughy cake laced with raisins and heavy with lard and sugar. Fortunately for my waistline, it proved inedible.

Oxford

I drove into Shakespeare country today, but determined to do nothing related to Shakespeare. Stratford-on-Avon lies in Warwickshire, my destination, but the web site for the Royal Shakespeare Company (rsc.uk.co) said that the troupe were not performing Shakespeare for the next few weeks, but instead an historical medley about English kings. That promised to be a sad tale, peppered with skullduggery, but, I had no need for dismal drama or an urge to peep at Anne Hathaway's chamber pot. I determined to skip the Shakespeare circuit altogether. Better luck next time, Bard.

Instead I headed straight for Oxford. Since, in my youth, long, long ago, I was a ten o'clock scholar reading matters of English language and literature, and since Oxford is home to many keepers of the tongue, it has long been a place of almost mythical import in my imagination. I must have read a hundred books on obscure topics in English Lit, all put out by the strange, crabbed, ardent scholars of Oxford. In my student days I actually wrote a letter to the editors of the

Oxford English Dictionary – an astonishing compendium of English language usage based on reading pretty much every darn thing written up to the 20th Century, and noting which texts presented first usage of words and how the meanings have evolved. In my letter, I scolded the chief editor for missing the true spelling of a somewhat arcane word, a catchall word that seldom pops up in conversation and only occasionally pops up in text. Your mistake, I explained to this bastion of the English language, is that you were careless and no doubt missing an important early text. The word commonly spelled "whatnot" is, undoubtedly, not based on a nonsensical combination of "what" and "not" but rather is based on the old English word meaning to know, "wot" and "not" -- and since the current usage of the word means "I know not what", it should be spelled "wotnot".

The OED editors did not write back.

By happy chance I entered the Oxford campus very near Magdalen (pronounced mawd-lun) College. I knew the place vaguely from books, because it was at Magdalen College that C.S. Lewis taught, and walking among the old buildings I spied gargoyles and statues on the roofs that might have been the inspiration for his Tales of Narnia. Magdalen College was also the place where Oscar Wilde slouched through school, taking honors and the cake. And at almost the same time, according to Tom Stoppard, A.E. Housman was attending Oxford, and squelching subterranean homosexual urges that Wilde was openly celebrating. A host of other characters from the bookish life hovered like ghosts just inside the gates.

I crossed the Cherwell Bridge approaching Magdalen. The Cherwell (pronounced Charwul) River is a small tributary of the Thames, which it joins at Oxford. Apparently, it's big enough to supply the college kids with sporting tradition.

The river was packed with rental boats beneath the bridge, but on this chilly spring day the boats had no takers. A boat-keeper in a loud striped shirt sulked below the bridge.

Walking along High Street I ducked into a café frequented by students, as evidenced by their vibrant faces and battered clothes. The menu was scrawled in chalk on a tiny blackboard behind the register, and for all I know it could have been the mathematical formula for the derivation of all prime numbers, but I picked out the phrase "small breakfast" – which I ordered – and was pleasantly surprised when it turned out to be fragrant coffee splashed with real cream and a buttered bun loaded with fried egg, tomatoes and a mound of salty bacon.

Munching and sipping I made my way past several mundane university buildings – administration stuff, health services, lecture hall -- and noticed that they were haphazardly sprinkled among buildings of the town of Oxford. Maybe this intermixture of the university buildings with bookstores and barber shops and mundane businesses was the cause of the famous friction between town and gown that led to a real riot in the14th or 15th Century, where students and townspeople were actually killing each other in the streets. On the day I visited, the students were cool.

The architecture of the university buildings held no surprises for me, because my own alma mater in Chicago was in the same style. My trusty guidebook (Lonely Planet, England, 1997, a gem) calls the style "perpendicular Gothic" but at the University of Chicago we called it "neoGothic". In both cases buildings featured heavy stone walls, occasionally decorated with coats of arms and gargoyles, topped by spires that were studded with nubby protrusions, just like the Houses of Parliament. The style was familiar but the color surprised me. In Chicago the university buildings are all a stately gray. Here the buildings were the color of yellowed parchment, or that buff leather called chamois.

I had meant to visit the Oxford University Publishing House museum, because it had an exhibit on the Oxford English Dictionary (which, if you care about such things, has a fascinating history of its own, including the fact that one its chief contributors, a brilliant lexicographer, was an American ex-physician who submitted many of his contributions, unknown to the Oxford scholars, from his cell in a prison for the criminally insane, where he in fact died, after cutting off his penis), but not 100 yards further down High Street I found a sign that said "Bodleian Library".

Now, if you are or were a scholar of the English language, you would realize that the Bodleian Library is the inner sanctum of the inner sanctum. A place where all book lovers go if they go to heaven – assuming that book lovers have a snowball's chance in Hell of going to heaven. A huge repository of books it is, and moreover a museum and curator and treasury of all things bibliophile. A passing guide leading a gaggle of tourists called the venerable old place "Victorian Gothic" -- which sounds like anachronism to me, but it may be the terminology in fashion just now. It had a quadrangular courtyard, with four doors in the four walls and each door bore an inscription in Latin of the name of the ancient branches of learning. The door that caught my eye was labeled <u>Schola Astronomie et Rhetoricae</u>, which pleased me because I like to see someone – even moldy, dust-laden, forgotten scholars – acknowledge the once exalted intellectual role of the art of rhetoric.

I paused just inside the entrance, ignoring the gift shop in favor of a small but exquisite anteroom. There were about half a dozen gray-haired men and women in long black robes gathered in the room, and more arriving each minute. I

143

realized it was some function for instructors, dons or masters as they are called at Oxford. They all looked like Mr. Chips in his academic gown. The ceiling of the small room was fretted with Gothic arches converging like petals of an onion bulb. The dons talked quietly; they emitted restrained but genuine laughter.

Back on the quadrangle I spotted a sign for an exhibit and I followed it to discover a roomful of glass cases containing incunabula. In my grad school days, I was taught that incunabula are the books created before the printing press – the huge, hand-lettered and beautifully illuminated texts created in medieval monasteries. But these books were early printed works. A poster told me that incunabula (Latin for swaddling clothes) were the earliest printed books, the ones dating from the 15th Century. Okay, if Oxford says so, I believe it.

One case held a Guttenberg Bible, one of only three that still reside in England today. It was as large as a rectangular pizza, had 42 lines per page and gilt edging on the paper. They reckon it was printed in 1455. Another case held an ethical treatise by a German ecclesiastic named Sebastian Brant. It was Das Narrenschiff (Ship of Fools), 1499. There were early books printed in Germany, France, Italy, and of course England. Apparently, in the 15th Century the printing industry took off like a rocket, and people everywhere were clamoring for more and more and more books. Compared to the flowering of intellect in that period of history, the so-called "Internet revolution" is little more than a bud.

It was well past noon before I reluctantly dragged myself away from Oxford, that bastion of the humanities – but I had promised myself a castle after lunch. I grabbed some cheese and bread for the car, because in England it is possible to munch and drive with one's knees, and in fact I think the practice is encouraged. Bidding Oxford a fond farewell (I'll be back) I zoomed off to castle grounds.

Warwick

Warwick Castle is one of the best-preserved ancient forts in all of England. It has become a popular tourist destination, in fact so popular that the ancient place was purchased by the Tussaud family in 1997 and, yes, it is filled with wax figures illustrating all the history that trod those castle walls.

The grounds of the place are huge. I was to wander later through vast green lawns and the back park with conservatory and stables, but even the walk up from the car park was impressive. It must take ten minutes to walk from the car to the castle entrance, and all along the way the grounds rustle from magnificent trees and exotic shrubs. From a distance you can make out stone towers, and closer you see pendants flying from the battlements and tents and oxcarts on an expansive lawn. I was reminded of a joke I heard probably fifty years ago when I sneaked downstairs, while my parents weren't looking, to overhear the late- night Jack Parr show. Parr told a story about a Texas millionaire who was visiting England and poo-pooing everything he saw. The roses were fine, but not as big as Texas roses. The castles were fine, but give me air-conditioning and shag carpet any day. His host asked if there was anything in England that he *did* find to his liking. The lawn, he said, was very nice. And he asked, "How do you get it like that?" His host replied that there was nothing to it. "One simply has one's people rake it every morning for two hundred years."

After paying a stiff entrance fee one walks up a small hill lined with brightly canopied tents – must be a colorful fake medieval fairgrounds in summer – over a small bridge spanning a now-dry moat, through the castle gates and high-walled entryway, from which boiling oil was probably dropped on invaders, to emerge on a huge courtyard lined all round with castle walls. Almost immediately you turn in at a doorway and plunge into the dungeon. Oddly enough, the dungeon and rack hold no wax figures writhing in waxen torment, but the display of spiked collars, thumbscrews, tooth wangers and ball busters is plenty grisly enough for even the most lurid tastes. We tourists try to imagine what it was like to have the spine snapped on the rack while the legs were being roasted. The mind flinches and we move on.

Entering the antechamber to the medieval living quarters, the first wax figure that caught my eye was a horse's ass. The tail twitched. Later I was to discover that a number of the manikins were mechanically automated, but that first one took me by surprise. Then followed a series of rooms filled with figures going about their daily medieval business. One room held an archer fletching arrows; another held an old maid doing laundry in a tub; another held a bejeweled treasurer and another a young girl playing a wooden flute. One table held cobbler's tools and another displayed chandler's molds. In a small corner, behind a curtain, stood a stone seat with a wooden toilet seat cover. No doubt this was serviced by a chamber pot, but I could not resist the image of aristocratic turds falling a hundred feet to the moat below. In the largest room the hereditary lords of the place, Earl of Warwick and his kith and kin held court. A gracious female figure draped in flowing silk combed her royal hair. The most famous Earl of Warwick was nicknamed "The Kingmaker", and he was instrumental in placing Henry I (or II or III) on the throne. The main thing I remember about the Warwick family that inhabited this castle for 500 years is that they are the ones who insisted on burning Joan of Arc. One of those earls confused a saint with a witch, or perhaps to the aristocracy, the two sorts of troublemaker were pretty much the same.

Emerging into the courtyard was refreshing. Nice lawn. Perhaps the product of 200 years raking. I took a quick walk up to the conservatory outside the castle walls. The jolliest feature was not the exotic blossoms inside the conservatory glasshouse but the children outside in the sunlight, stalking and whooping at the covey of eight peacocks trying to catch a nap in the afternoon sun. I got a gulp of chilly air and a flash of blue sky before I returned to the castle proper and plunged into the next set of rooms.

A small family chapel outside the reception area (great hall) had pastel stained-glass windows and a magnificent carved wood altar. At the back of The Great Hall stood suits of armor and the walls held portraits of various earls and earlesses and earlettes. In a corner stood a huge iron cauldron that held, according to a recipe on the wall, "18 gallons brandy, 18 gallons rum, 100 gallons water, lemon and sugar in proportion" as prepared for entertaining at the birth of the umteenth Earl of Warwick. The sign said that at one Christmas feast it was filled four times. Another display that held me was a glass case that contained, it claimed, the saddle of Queen Elizabeth. Imagine that, the leather and fabric from 1592 that supported the queen's bum, right there for all to see.

Then down a long hallway which opened into rooms crammed with aristocratic bric-a-brac, four-poster beds trimmed in blue silk and ornate lamps and gorgeous carved stone fireplaces. Then past a suite of rooms holding old swords and ornamental cannon. A model torso was dressed in light armor called "brigantine" which consisted of iron plates attached to a silk blouse. There followed yet another expanse of rooms which contained the "modern" or 19th Century décor. A friendly guide dressed in formal black introduced herself as "Lady Pamela", and she explained that the rooms we were about to view depicted the Victorian period of the Castle. Sure enough, there followed room after room decked out in Victorian finery – heavy damask curtains and "modern" appliances like the gramophone, plush chairs with carved lion's feet next to dark mahogany tables inlaid with mother-of-pearl, china and oils and tapestries galore. The library did not contain Colonel Mustard with a lead pipe but instead a wax figure of the Edwardian Earl smoking a wax cigar. One room had a figure of the young Winston Churchill, a frequent guest in the castle while he was an up and coming politico, and another room had an image of the slightly portly king-to-be, Prince Edward. One room was all decked out in the latest fad -- elegant fake Chinese furnishings including a bed with a pagoda atop the four-posts.

Lady Pamela explained to us that the family sold the castle to the Tussaud family in 1998, after failing for years to meet the tax burden and upkeep for the huge estate. Lady Pamela was an actress, of course, hired to murmur interesting facts about Victorian life in the ears of passing tourists, but she seemed genuinely dismayed to report that the castle was no longer in the hands of the lords and ladies. As we say in Oxford, *sic transit gloria mundi*.

My favorite part of the tour was visiting the power mill below the castle walls on the River Avon. At the turn of the century, when indoor electrical lighting was still an experiment in luxury, the reigning earl had the old gristmill down on the river converted from grinding grain to turning a generator. The lady of the castle threw a great Powder Ball in 1894 where the gentry dressed in powdered wigs and chiffon gowns danced the night away under the glow of (ooo-la-la) electric chandeliers.

Although the mill had been in operation for centuries, and in fact was used to grind grain for the royalist soldiers during the 17th Century Civil War, it had been largely replaced by city services in Victorian times. The restoration done in the late 1960's preserved the primitive dynamos, the huge gears, the 20-foot long leather drive belts, and all. It was such a massive, crude setup that it illustrated the basics of power generation like a child's storybook. I was fascinated to observe that the mill-keepers (called engineers in the power generation era) kept an eel trap down by the water wheel. Trapping eels was an ancient privilege of the millers, and in fact their produce was often served in the castle dining hall as a great delicacy, even during the dead of winter, since, although eels hibernate during the coldest months, a few were still brought up all winter long and easily preserved on river ice.

The great water wheel turned on a multi-ton axel that drove a series of gears to step up the rotation to about 3000 rpm as required by the bulky 19th Century generators. The gears were connected to the generator spindles by long leather belts. Originally the belts were made of tanned giraffe neck, the only substance with the length and durability to satisfy the need. Thank heavens that barbaric practice has now been discontinued. As I understand it, today the belts are made from tanned tourist necks – commoners of the rubber-necking disposition.

By the time I left the power mill it was early dusk. The long climb up from the river left no time to visit the gift shop, but I detoured before returning to the car park to wander among the shops along the narrow, cobbled streets of the ancient village of Warwick. Today it contains mobile phone shops, unisex hair parlors and such – the sort of thing that would have had a previous earl burn the place to the ground for witchcraft. I got a box of Belgian chocolates at a little shop just off the main road. I asked the proprietor what he thought of the ancient castle up on the hill. "A nuisance to drive around," he said. And he never went there, he said, and in fact no one from Warwick cared a fig to see the castle. "However," he said, smiling as he handed me change from a 10-pound note, "it does bring the crowds."

Stonehenge

Blue sky on this Saturday morning. I was up early and noticed that the birds in the nearby woods had changed from magpies to robins. Spring imminent, I guess, but too chill and quiet to mean much. I had meant to get an early start but dawdled over coffee and by the time I hit the highway it was 9:30 and turning colder. Driving west from Basingstoke, the small villages gave way to gently sloping farmland. Nothing much planted yet, but the fields were tidy and clean. Here and there a flock of grazing sheep like dirty clouds.

Stonehenge is in the middle of nowhere – or to be more precise, in the middle of Salisbury Plain, a large flat sheet of nondescript farmland a hundred miles west of London. It's odd that such a renowned place, a place once high and holy perhaps, should lie so far from the rivers or fords or ports or fertile marshes that usually accompany ancient cities. But this place was always remote, nowadays just a curio at the intersection of two minor highways, and from the looks of it, the locale of Stonehenge had always been strange and desolate. When I emerged from the warm car, the air clouded with my breath. The reception center was alive with ravens and starlings, attracted by the bun crumbs thrown by tourists.

You don't need me to describe Stonehenge. It looks like the pictures. It's just a bunch of huge stone slabs set on end with more stone slabs laid horizontally on top. The scene could be colossal building blocks, or Paul Bunyan's dominos. On closer examination you notice hammer marks – stone maul marks – banged into the stone. You notice that one boulder, bare on top with the lintel missing, has a protruding tit of stone that must have held the lintel in place like a mortise and tenon joint. The stones are set in a rough circle, with an inner horseshoe-shaped row of smaller "blue stones" and outside the circle a trench about six feet wide. Looking up to the horizon, you notice mounds in the distance, some bare, some grassy, and none very impressive, just buboes on the flanks of Earth.

The voice droning in my ear from the free audio guide to Stonehenge tells me that the mounds were barrows, ancient burial sites which can be found all over England and are particularly commonplace in this remote spot. Digs in the barrows turn up pretty much what you would expect: old bones, crude jewelry, stone implements, pot shards. Just exactly the sort of stuff we find back home in the Cahokia Mounds, where the ancient Indigenes made a large community burial ground. The difference perhaps is that this site was a Stone Age gathering place 5000 years ago. The Stone Age folk in the new world, without metal or glass or the wheel, gathered in Cahokia about 600 years ago. But they were akin, much like you and me, possessing a vague, powerful need to show respect for the dead.

I stood for many minutes in the chilly morning breeze, staring at the great silent stones. The silence is part of their appeal. The lonely, wind-swept plain is likewise taciturn to a fault. Nothing ought to be in that desolate place, and yet there they stand, a huge brute fact, a monumental -- and by all standards today -- nonsensical testament to something or other. The voice in my ear says that the largest stone weighs 45 tons and that hauling it here from quarries in Wales and digging a sloping trench with which to erect it would have taken 600 men weeks or months. And the question rises like mist on the cold air: why? For pity's sake why put this monstrous clump of rocks in this place? What was going on 5000 years ago that could motivate or justify such a huge undertaking?

Nobody knows what Stonehenge is all about, according to my audio guide. The popular theories on close examination get blown to smithereens. It was not a Druid worship site, they say, since the Romans arrived 3000 years after the stones were set up and discovered the funky Druids, miserably disorganized, worshipping in forest glens. No high pagan mass in this treeless plain. Some archeologists point out that the arrangement of stones forms a calendar, with June falling between two slabs, July between the next two, August the next, and so on. But that is just a theory, and the stones alignment has to be fudged a bit to jibe with the astronomic facts. And the place hosted no human sacrifice, probably no sacrifice at all, since the theory that certain flat stones were altars was taken from the mundane fact that some of the fallen stone contain iron traces and turn reddish after centuries of rain. Not blood stains; just plain old rust. Tus, the New Age theories of Stonehenge are mostly hooey. What it was and why it was remain a mystery.

I returned to my car to sip hot chocolate and try to puzzle it out. No explanation quite fits. The only thing I know about Stonehenge is that in early March the place is solemn, austere, haunting, and cold enough to freeze your teeth.

Bath

The drive to Bath presented more rolling hills, flocks of sheep, and trim hedge rows that in half an hour turned downright woodsy. Pines appeared, and then clumps of oak signifying mature forest. I had always imagined that England was devoid of forest, maybe all chopped down for steam engine fuel – that the adoration of trees that emerges from the novels of JRR Tolkien was like the flower fetish of the Swedish playwright August Strindberg, who can make you feel that a rosebud, after a cruel Swedish winter, is something rare and holy – but no, the English countryside was not denuded but positively amuck with root and branch. Tolkien must just like trees.

As you enter Bath (pronounced Baaath), you descend to a bend in the River Avon (as in Stratford-on) and travel in time, passing through four cultures. At the perimeter is the modern city – the row houses and railways and (god help us) gaudily lit strip malls. Descending the river valley walls, you come upon the Georgian period, the 19th Century's elegant yellow stone homes, built when this was the cat's pajamas, the most elegant city in the world, the place where everybody who was anybody (English) simply had to go to see and be seen, to sport the latest fashions, eat the finest foods, and of course, take the cure. Still further down, on the river floor, you encounter the old Roman town, the remnants of times when the invader army built the sulfur springs into a place for worship, socializing, and of course, bathing. (I omit the medieval culture, since every ancient English town has its churches and market streets and blessed virgin fountains, usually built on Roman ruins, and often with no great improvement). Then finally, down at the river itself, you spy the crooked streets, the old stone walls and bridges that Saxons built before Rome arrived and simultaneously clobbered and urbanized everything.

The main attraction is the Roman bath smack in the middle of the old town. Large yellow stone buildings like temples (which they were) or forums (which they were) or bathhouses (which they could still be, since the springs still gush and bubble madly in the pool, but since the joint has become a museum and tourist Mecca, no one bathes). Entering a long hallway in the museum, you gawk at various relics as you parade down to poolside. The room is studded with display cases holding fragments of stone columns, pediment statuary, old coins fished from the pool, a few Roman bobby-pins and preserved sandal fragments. Although the Romans built baths in nearly every town they conquered, the baths at Bath were considered sacred. Discovering hot, medicinal water gushing from the bowels of the Earth was, probably to the local bumpkins and the Romans alike, a sign of the gods. Pediment bas relief suggests that the baths housed temples to various deities – Apollo, Mercury, Minerva, and some more primitive fellow who has snakes for a beard. One bas relief depicts a god dangling a lazy foot over the rim of heaven, I suppose, and beside him a globe representing the world below. I note that the world is shown as a globe, not flat, but round, and that this artifact was sculpted 1500 years before Columbus.

The Roman bath featured a carefully controlled mix of warmth and water. The idea evolved over the centuries into what we know today as a "Turkish bath". The place had separate rooms for changing and massage and getting an oil rubdown -- even a place for slaves to scrape the skin of oil. It had warming rooms, a very hot chamber, the bubbly smelly bath itself, and then a place for a cold plunge. Romans often spent the whole day at the bath, washing of course, but also dining, gambling, conducting business, and no doubt flirting.

Curators have created a number of intriguing displays of Roman engineering. Romans used hollow "bricks" made of molded terra cotta to create insulating spaces. The place was roofed, for use in winter, and the thick marble base of the walls was transformed higher up into brick arches which eventually gave way to the light hollow brick to seal the space. In the hottest room the floor was raised on pedestals of brick, and hot air was introduced from a furnace adjoining. The hot air warmed the floor (people wore wooden sandals) and it passed upward through the hollow-brick wall where it was released as steam into the cooler night air. The bath itself started as a hot spring, but the Romans fed it to a reservoir that flowed into a lead-lined marble pool, creating a controlled and elegant 20x40 foot bubbling bath. The lead lining remains in place and perfectly functional still, 2000 years later.

The walls are stained brownish-yellow about four feet above the pool level. Museum notes explain that in medieval times the ruined baths were taken over by the Church and the water level raised, so that there would be footing and space to allow lepers to come and get cleansed and possibly a cure. Later, English kings tore down the infrastructure to allow the bath to return to its classical levels, but the sulfur stain remains.

On the way out, one is invited to take refreshment in the elegant Victorian dining saloon above the bath, a place called the Pump Room. Spring water is pumped up to this establishment and guests are encouraged to drink a glass or two of the miracle water which is "good for what ails ya". In Chicago there's a fancy restaurant that's called the Pump Room, and I bet it is named after this joint – minus the pump. But I declined to sip on my way out, having no taste for stinky water and no need for a cure. In fact, the murky glass of fluid at the fountain seemed about as appetizing as a leper's French kiss.

During the drive home, as evening settled like a mantle over the quiet English countryside and headlights on autos thronging the M3 Highway popped on, an idea popped into my head. Stonehenge, Bath, only thirty miles distant and yet worlds apart and yet maybe not so far apart. Aha! I cried (well not really, because I was driving with my knees on the left side of the highway and munching Carr's cheese crackers). Maybe, indeed, there was a connection! Maybe it was like Delphi, the high holy place on Mount Parnassus in Greece. I recalled an article in Scientific American that dealt with Delphi, site of the ancient Oracle situated above a sacred hot spring. The authors noted that there is evidence to suggest that the priestess of Delphi sat over an opening in the Earth which spewed noxious fumes, possibly naturally occurring ethylene, which induced a trance that led to mystical visions and prophecy.

And here, not so far from the hot springs of Bath, was a similar mystical site. Stonehenge, perhaps like Delphi, had long since lost its sulfur spring and lost its appeal as a place of holy revelation, but that secret spring might have been the basis of its reputation. The more I thought about it, the more I liked the idea. Call it the Ethylene Theory of Antiquity. The theory, I saw at once, was virtually unassailable because it was based on not a shred of evidence.

Perhaps the Ethylene Theory of Antiquity could be expanded to account for a number of ancient mysteries – Atlantis, Easter Island, the Leaning Tower of Pisa, Nostradamus and, of course, the Trojan Horse. All these strange works have a similar source. Not the work of alien overlords, not the creations of giants or geniuses, but rather the work of ancient people possessed of curiosity, skills, and inspiration. Only, compared to us, they were, more deeply and persistently, zonked.

Portsmouth

On Sunday I got a hankering to see the sea, so I headed south toward the nearest coastline and found the ancient shipyard and bustling modern city of Portsmouth. After the usual wrong turns and accidental tourism, I parked at a bustling shopping center called Gunwale Quay. Unwisely I stopped and ordered a Whopper for lunch – part nourishment and part cure for homesickness. The meal was unwise because the nourishment was dubious and the faintly alien taste of British ketchup only accentuated the homesickness.

You pay a modest base fee just to enter the "historical dockyard", and I chose two attractions: HMS Victory and the Royal Naval Museum for a total of 9.75 GBP ($20). The Victory tour didn't begin for an hour, so I ducked into the museum. The place was crammed with predictable memorabilia – old anchors, ships' bells, models and pendants and nautical paraphernalia. My curiosity was piqued by a glass case just past the entrance. It contained several nifty model ships, and when I looked more closely I found that they were made, spars, decks, rudder and all, from carved ivory. A note in the case explained that these ships were made by French sailors who were prisoners of war in the clashes of Limeys and Frogs during the 1760's. They carved the models from soup bones, beef and mutton slops they were fed as prisoners. Next to the carved ships lay some fine pieces of lace – also manufacture of the prisoners. A sign above the lace stated that local English craftswomen complained that the sailors' work was better quality and sold much cheaper than their own stock-in-trade, at which time the trade was abolished.

One of the first displays concerned naval food supplies. A fairly jingoish poster explained that England emerged at the Ruler of the Seas thanks in large part to better organization ashore. The common fare of the English sailor (unless they were very long at sea) included biscuits, beans, salt pork and "56 pints of beer per man per week." Another poster by the famous 17th Century diarist Samuel Pepys stated that "Englishmen and more specially seamen love their bellies above anything else. --1686"

I grazed at displays of various naval knickknacks: plastic hardtack with plastic weevils, a case of campaign medals, old swords and epaulets and such claptrap. A few displays were "action stations" where I reefed a sail and fired a simulated cannon. The Brits call a square knot a "reef knot". By the time I finished blasting a few pirates of the Caribbean, it was time to tour the H.M.S. Victory.

H.M.S. Victory is, according to the posters displayed beside the entrance queue, the most famous ship in the world. The English certainly love their history. It was the flagship of Lord Admiral Nelson, the fellow who commanded the British fleet at the Battle of Trafalgar, when the English soundly trounced a fleet of French and Spanish ships, thereby ending a threat of invasion by the forces of Napoleon Bonaparte and proving to the world that "Britannia rules the waves".

We explored nearly every section of the ship, from the main deck and rigging on the mizzenmast (the rear pole), to the hold and the leather-lined powder store. We gawked at cannons and galleys and water barrels stacked on gravel in the hold. We stood on the quarterdeck where Nelson was struck by a musket ball fired by a sailor in the rigging of a nearby French ship. There's a little brass plaque on the spot where he fell. He was carried below decks to the surgeon's area (normally the mess hall when not in battle) and he died three hours later. We visited the place where he died and learned from the guide that every year on the battle anniversary, October 21st, the big cheeses of the Admiralty gather there to drink a toast to the long-dead hero. The battle occurred in 1805, and for more than 200 years people from all over the world – and the Brits especially – have gathered in Portsmouth to celebrate that victory and that hero. Shakespeare wrote that "the evil men do lives long after them while the good is oft interred with their bones." But not always, not in England.

Below decks I was fascinated by the brig, the onboard prison. Times were hard aboard ship – weevils in the hardtack, brinish water to drink, 800 men living in extremely close quarters and sharing it with the pigs, sheep and other livestock brought aboard for fresh meat. Sometimes sailors misbehaved, and sometimes they were slung into the brig.

We tourists saw the leg irons where a man was bound, awaiting punishment. A sailor would be instructed to unravel part-way a six-foot length of thick manila rope, leaving nine strands of rope knotted at the end. This was the infamous "cat-o-nine-tails". The prisoner would place the sturdy whip into a special canvas bag. The sailor sat 24 hours in leg irons, and come the dawn he would be taken to the main deck, because below deck "there wasn't room to swing a cat". The cat would be taken out of the bag, and the flogging would begin. The usual punishment was 12 lashes, which was enough to take the flesh off a man's back. For serious crimes, a man might receive 48 lashes – enough to kill a sick or weak man.

Surprisingly, most of the men aboard ship were conscripts. (I know something about that condition, myself having been conscripted into the U.S. Army to serve in southern Vietnam back in the days of our amateur Army.) During the Battle of Trafalgar, 821 men served aboard the Victory and over 60% were "pressed" into service. Some men were tricked into signing sailing orders, some were conked on the head in a honky-tonk, and woke up bound for Shanghai. A man might be drinking ashore and have some ensign slip a coin into his mug of beer. If he reached the bottom of the mug and fished out the coin, he was said to have "accepted the king's sovereign" and legally he was bound to serve on the ship.

That practice gave rise to the custom of serving beer in glass-bottomed mugs.

What to make of those pressed men, wrenched from their homes, families, and jobs and then forced to work like slaves aboard a creaking ship that faced fearful storms, gun battles and strange disease? The sailors were virtually imprisoned without trial, without committing a crime, but rather to serve the nation at a time of crisis, and this injustice might have provoked outrage. And yet, it seems, it did not..

There is something ironic, and maybe sweetly idiotic, in the way people shrug off hardship in the face necessity. After being so ill-used, after years at sea, far from home and family, after pirates and malaria and the doldrums, sailors came ashore and bragged about their service in the Queen's Navy. Those who made it back home from Trafalgar, I suspect, would not have traded that experience for the world. Thus does time transmute the miseries of youth into the fond memories of age.

With that thought, I left the shores of England.

The View from Across the Pond

Returning home from these jaunts to Europe, I reflect that either the world is shrinking or my mind is expanding. Or both. The globe is a shrunken head of its former self.

Europe and the larger world, just a generation or two ago, seemed remote, almost inaccessible, sophisticated and steeped in romance. We Americans mooned over palace gardens in Versailles and cathedrals in Venice – not to mention temples in Siam and the markets of far Cathay. People wrote songs about "faraway places with strange-sounding names," and decorated their apartment walls with posters of bull fights in Lisbon and sunsets in Ceylon. Today, however, with cheap jet travel and the Internet, both our ignorance and our romance have largely evaporated. The planet seems much smaller today than it did just ten years ago, when the melting of polar icecaps seemed irrelevant to the wild fires of California. A generation ago we might dismiss Latin American politics as "banana republic" turmoil, but today we digest it with dinner and the nightly news. The woes of the world – flooding, crop failure, mass migrations, petty wars and epidemics – wash over us like neighborhood gossip. And because everything impacts us, too often nothing much touches us.

As an antidote, I recommend travel. The trouble with our modern televised and homogenized culture is that we get only crumbs of reality. We see only summaries, digests, the fleeting images and glossy surface of things. On television, Italy blends into France which resembles England which looks like Germany. All Europeans look alike. Streaming travelogues and documentaries make foreign lands more familiar and, as the saying goes, "familiarity breeds contempt". Virtual travel provides a gloss of the real thing, whereas being there – if only the smattering of countries that I have visited – being on the ground, walking cobblestone lanes, smelling fresh laundry and tasting the wine, startles us with the complexity of reality. For me, at the right place and in the nick of time, it rescues the romance.

Made in the USA
Las Vegas, NV
27 October 2020

10368488R00090